Along Life's Road

Book 2

Poetry, Songs and Stories

Written By Albert E. Vicent
Compiled By Haruka Vicent
And Michael Vicent
Cover Photo By Albert C. Vicent

Order this book online at www.trafford.com
or email orders@trafford.com

Most Trafford titles are also available at major online book retailers.

Print information available on the last page.

ISBN: 978-1-4907-7090-1 (sc)
ISBN: 978-1-4907-7089-5 (e)

Trafford rev. 02/25/2016

 www.trafford.com

North America & international
toll-free: 1 888 232 4444 (USA & Canada)
fax: 812 355 4082

Along

Along the road
We touch
We see
We feel
We gaze
At the beauty
The wonders
The new
The old
The past
And future
Along the road
Along the road
Of life.

Table of Contents

Poems

Song

Story

About the Author

Poems

Strange

Now that you appreciate me
Now that I appreciate you
We can together see
We don't have to
Fight each other
We can do most all
Things together
There's love in you
You see love in me
There's things you do
I like
There's things I do
You like
We can more forward
Together
Now that you appreciate me
Now, that I appreciate you
Isn't it strange
Why didn't we see that before
Isn't it strange ?

Fun

When you're painting
With brushes
Maybe one-or two
And you're mopping
With a mop
With water too
And you are three
Or four or five
Years old.
Or a little more.
Everywhere you paint
And mop the floor
Looks really really
New and clean
Not old anymore.
Cause when you're
Painting and mopping
That's so much fun to do.
If you try it
You, might like too.

Of Snow

Mountain tops of snow
Soon to melt and go
Left from cool of night and day
Soon too disappear, away
Now...
Make beautiful
To watch and see
Where far away
They stay-they be
Mountain tops of snow
Mountain tops of cold
Mountain tops of snow.

Me

I want to see me
Where is me
What happened to me
Where can I aim
To be the same
As before
I want more of me
I seem to have lost me
I want to see me
Where is me
What happened,
To me.

A Bear

When you run and run and run
From a bear
And you turn a corner
And the bear
Shakes hands with you
What do you do
Do you run and run-again
Or disappear,
To another land
No...
Don´t feel bad-or
Be too sad
Others have done this
To bears they´ve seen
Too
As they pass this way
Going thru
And bears wonder
Why
As others run and run and run
From a bear.

Wide Open Sea

Oh the sea, the sea
The wide open sea
By day there´s no signs
Or by night to guide
Save light houses
Near shores-to see,
Oh the sea, the sea
Oh the wide open sea
Only knowledge
Only knowledge
In the guide-there be.
So...
Be careful
Be careful
On the wide open sea,
It swallows
and covers
Claims...Silently.
The sea-the sea
The wide open sea.

A Greeting

A hello is a greeting
And a way to start
The day in a beautiful way
A hand shake
And a smile too
Permeates thru
Mixing, communicating, leading
In many ways
Thru a world that
Gives beauty
Has hills, small, large
Mountains of tall
Far away close
Purple with haze
With clouds, sunshine too
And also a creation
With rainbows of
Colors lovely-and of
Sunshine, moonlight, starlight
Given freely with love
Having traveled thru
This creation
Witnessed the beauty
Climbed the mountains-conquered
Waved a victory, left memories
Communicated-my way...
Loved and raised a family
To friends and all, now
With my leaving
As of a sunset lovely,
Consider
A hello to evening...
And love-to sunrise.

Cloud Cover

The clouds are coming
The clouds are coming
I know they are coming
I see the clouds coming
Now...
There´s blue in the sky to see
But the clouds are going
Where ever they please
They´re starting way over there
Over the top of the top of the-
Far away trees
And soon they´ll cover
The blue in the sky
And they will be-then soon,
All over the sky
The clouds are coming
The clouds are coming
I know they are coming
To cover...
To cover the sky.
What can we do?
The clouds are coming
The clouds are coming.

Pass Thru

So beautiful
To help-where needed
And most do
As special days
Pass thru
But when the special
Time has passed
The need remains
The need-it lasts
So beautiful to help
Where needed
As needs,
Pass thru.

Sky of Blue

One cloud only
In a big sky of blue
Drifting this way
That way too.
Where will it go
And what will it do
And how will it know
When it gets
Where its going to
Should a soft breeze
Help it-
On its way.
Or best, let it drift
Go where it may.
One cloud only
One cloud only
One cloud only
In a big sky of blue.
We are watching you
One cloud only
To see what
You do.

Storm

After a wintry storm
And tree branches are-
Heavy laden with ice and snow
Some branches break-
From the body of the tree
Fall, let go.
Then from warmth of
Daily sun-the tree
Continues to grow
"Eternal life" continues after storms
Wintry storms pass
And go.

The Year

Days and daze and then
Holidays
Kind of make up the year
In on orderly way.
Of course there's the weather
And birds of feather
Then sunshine, clouds
Rainbows too.
Now they add beauty
To the sky
Which at night
With stars of bright
With moonlight also
On silent nights
Where a distant animal
Can sing with talent given
Ring
Thru distance far
Why nature beautiful
In just lovely ways
Contributes
Eternally
To our
Days and daze and then
Holidays.

All Blue

The sky is blue
All blue today
Oh no there is
One white cloud
Over that house
Far away.
Now-
If that cloud
Would go away
The sky would be
All blue today.

Today

Dec 7th reaches thru
And touches
In a way,
And lives-and dies
Survives
And has a way.
That means and makes
True history live
To some-
In love-with love.
In strange,
But
Understanding...
Yet, very personal
Ways.
And life-goes on...Today-
And everyday.

Humanity

Peace must be
For all humanity
To survive
And be-
Forever reside
With love
For all
Peace must reign
Or all
Matters not
Where´re
The country be
For all to-
Lovely be
Peace must be.

Talk

Talking talking
Talking
Even if no one
Is near
Talking brings out the beautiful
Brings the unseen
So near.
To talk
Brings out the lovely
Talking creates
Memories
That forever
In love
Stay near.

Gift

A gift, a gift, a gift to give
What would you give
To make world- a better place
A better place to live
Would you give food-food to eat
Would you give a home
A place to roam
Would you give good health
So all could more healthy be
Would you give good schools
So good education could rule
Would you stop wars
So peace could reign
Neath far off stars
What would be-
The greatest gift
That you would give
To make this world
A better place to live.

Calm

The rain came down
And the wind it blew
Intermittent at times
Then ferocious sometime
The sun would show
The moon would too
For days it seemed
The storm continued
Then came a calm
And all was strange
For once honesty came
When no storm remained
For all needed it seemed
Storms to be, for all to see-
A need to be.
Quite strange some be
That rain must fall
For the sun to see,
And calm to be.

A Passing Cloud

A passing cloud,
Dropped rain from the sky.
The rain fell on people,
Both you and I.
That a passing cloud
So high in the sky,
Should drop,
Rain from the heavens
Oh you and I.
Is,
A blessing from God.
Who rules,
Earth,
Heaven
And sky.

Layered

A 3 layered cake
Now that's-what I'd
Like to see
A 3 layered cake
I wonder-
If that could ever be
Maybe lots of folk,
Would like it
If a cake like that
They'd see.
A 3 layered cake
Now, that's what-
I'd like to see.

Ordinary

Another ordinary day
When things of good
Come our way
Not the entirely
Unusual.
But the necessary
Eye opening lovely
Are there in beautiful
Ways.
Another ordinary day
Given with love
When things of good
Come our way.

Gotta Watch

The boys, the boys
The boys said
The dinosaurs ate
All the rabbits
And all squirrels too.
They said the dinosaurs
Do this
When the dinosaurs
Come thru.
And the boys said-they said
The dinosaurs don't ride
Skateboards, bicycles
They don't drive cars.
But, the dinosaurs
Take big steps-when they walk
That take then very far.
And don't forget,
They also eat-
Squirrels and rabbits too.
So, you really gotta
Watch-dinosaurs...
When they, come thru.

By-By

The sun is going
By-by
The children-they told me so
I'll watch the sun
From here below.
Right here-till twilight time.
And when the sun goes
By, by.
I'll see the sun...
At by, by-
Time.

There's Today

Way past the sea
Up next to the sky
Where soft the hours
Just drift- slow by
And the sky is crystal blue
Reflecting quiet
With beauty thru
To each day- especially today
Cause...
Soft the hours- just drift today
As the heavens
Send love
In most beautiful
Lovely ways
Look... yes look
Way past the sea
Up next to the sky
And...
There's today.

With me

Would you please
Just come and
Talk with me
I'm lonesome, lonesome
As can be
For nobody comes
To my house
To talk with me
Would you please
Just talk, talk, talk
To me
Would you please come
Talk, talk to me
Would you please come
Talkitty talkitty talk
Would you please
Just come and
Talk, talk with me
And see the things
I see
That talk my way
With me.

Birds

Birds standing on the church
Rooftop
Many do I see,
Closer to heaven-maybe
Are they,
Than-
Perhaps...
Are we.

Christmas

Red cookies
Green cookies
Blue cookies
Purple cookies
Yellow cookies
Orange cookies
Christmas cookies
Its Christmas season now
And today the children made
Cookies-
Christmas cookies.

Remember

Wherever you go
Whatever you do
With life try best
To flow
With the good, the bad-
The best.
As it comes-as it leaves
As it stays
And always remember
Love.
For love always
As the heaven above
Thru faith, offers-forgiveness
True comfort-hope
Beautiful-eternal and the lovely
Wherever you go
Whatever you do
Always-remember...
Love.

Blue Sky

The sky is blue today
All over very blue today
Down to the tree tops
Blue
Down to the hilltops
Too
No clouds in the sky
Today
The sky is all over
Blue
I like the blue sky
And the way it is today
All really really blue
With bright, bright
Of
Sunshine
Too.

Happy Cheer

Thanksgiving day´s finished
The day after too
And Sunday´s half way-finished
Soon be gone too
Just few more days
December will be here-meaning...
Christmas will be on its way
The holidays-oh the holidays
Are on their way.
Someplace with snow,
Snow men, snowballs and all
Someplace sunshine all day long
But when holidays arrive with
Tinkling bells decorations too
Happiness, sorrow, smiles, anticipation
Comes long beautiful too
And in a special way
That seems only to be
When the holiday of Christmas
We tend to see-to feel
Its way
Right after thanksgiving day´s
Finished
And December's here
With its special wintry,
Chilly, sunshine-years finish
But happy-
With...
Cheer.

The Crow

So soft-so soft
The crow flies by.
One can see, but hear it?
No...
Not I.

The Tree

Just adding another
Blossom to a tree
After a winter
That was cold
From a source we can't see.
Adds beauty to lives
Adds beauty to the tree
Thru love
For love
From a love
Greater- then we
Just by adding
Another
Eternal... blossom
To the tree.

Fundraiser

Today we had
A fundraiser at
Our church today
People came
To see, to buy
To pick up things at
The fundraiser we had
At our church today
Do you belong to a church?
Do you have fundraisers
At your church?
Fundraisers helps a church
Raise funds
We had a fundraiser
At our church today.

Was Spring

And it was spring
Breezes blew
Love grew
Soft winds
And love was all about
Blossoms came
To trees of green
Grass it grew
Filled valleys
Hills and dales
While flowers of wild
Grew with beauty
Filled all around
As nights moonlight rays
With silent lovely
Appeared
For it was spring
Breezes
Soft beautiful blew
And silently
Love lovely simply lovely was
Felt thru birth
A wonder in the spring
Of new, new life.

Grew

On the ocean
The sun and the waves
How they dance
And they shine
Thru the days
As they play
Under skies that are blue
And on the land
Not ocean
Green grass grew.

Different

I am me-you are you
we think different to
I see far-maybe
you see, more far.
maybe
I see high-you see low
maybe
you see sunshine
I see far
maybe you think near
I think far
that really make's we-and
the world different
because we are
different
in how we think
we are
and...
that's good.
that helps
to make the world,
Different– too.

Mysteries

Some things
in a picture-you may see
that you don't know
from long ago
may seem a mystery
and perhaps its better
let it remain that way
its nice to have
some
mysteries
too of,
long ago.

Able

No matter
how deep
no matter
how high
no matter
how wide
no matter what
If…
we leave
the entire
matter
up to the
creator
the creator
is always
able-to
oversee the
entire matter
and-plan
and...
can.

The Wind

Yesterday,
when the wind blew
thru
the trees did sway
autumns leaves
they flew
people bent low
and kind of-walked
in to the wind
some chairs out side
even moved some
too
the wind really blew
yesterday...
When the wind
blew-thru.

Slumber

Dreams are
usually nice
and give us something
to think about
too
they're usually of
something we've seen
thought about
and in some way
remember-while we
slumber
then mixed-and
produce in the dream
dreams...
Give us something
to think about
they do.

November

When the month
of November
passes thru
and its in the evening
while outside golden crispy leaves
are drifting down
its nice to settle in
a nice soft comfy chair
and sit-and let
a quiet November
Evening pass-
then soon,
thanksgiving day
Passes
just lovely
thru.

Focus

When things get
real rough
on life's sometimes
stormy seas.
focus on one thing
like the son
above
and be guided thru
with,
eternal love.

You

Hey, hey, hey man
hey man you
ain't no toilet
here for you
you homeless man
I'm talking bout you.
Public toilets-ain't none too
sorry man, kinda sorry
for you
hey, hey, hey man
hey man you.

Sunshine

You light up my life
A special way
Like sunshine does
When it shines
Each day
Then the days they fly
Good thoughts
Pass by
When I think of you
Or I even try.
You light my life
You light up my life
A special way
Every day-every day.
Every...single day.

Danced

They danced they danced
They danced at our school today
The young folks danced
They danced a break dance
They rolled on the floor
They kicked on the floor
They done a cheerleader dance
They danced more more
The older folks
They danced some too
But soon they were thru
All had a good time
When they danced today
They danced they danced
At the talent show
They danced they danced
Many dances
A good many dances
The children and all
When they danced their dances
At our school today

Light

The mornings are beautiful
For they come in a way
As light from above
And flowers of love
That flows soft
On pillars of light
And awakens the world
A special way
From dark- to the light of day.
Meaningful- beautiful
Comforting and silently
As a river flows
Memorably on.
Beautiful as from the start
Like light from above
With care...
With love.
The mornings are beautiful.

Pounds

It seems that
No matter- what you do
No matter how hard
You try
The pounds come on
As the years go by
The food tastes good
You sit.
When you stood
Then...
You stretch- round,
The waist
And it takes more food
Just- to fill up the space
Then you get a little
Larger too.
It seems that
No matter what you do
No matter how you try
The pounds come on
As the years
Go by.

Old Friends

Finding looking up
Old friends
Of long ago
Is like finding
Snow, from winter
In summer
Now, just where
Did it go?
Unless, its like ice
A little of
What it was long ago.
But if its water
Its easy to scatter
So its hard
To know.
Finding old friends
From long ago
Its hard to know
Just where
To go- at least,
Seems so.

Wide Range

Isn't life strange
Life covers a wide, wide, range
Those we thought- not our friends
Become friends thru ways
Of strange.
Even thru war at times
Later
Strangers become family lifetime friends
With love- true love...
Have families, sometime,
Lots of time.
Love each others countries
For lifetimes- lifetimes, after
Isn't life strange...
Life covers a wide, wide, range.

Of Night

In the late of night
When its nearly morning
Its just as quiet
As quiet can almost be
For it seems
All is quiet
Except some noise...darkness,
Which can't sleep
Quietly
In the late of night
When its just as quiet
As quiet
Can almost...
Be.

Buzzard Tree

Oh my way to work
Everyday
I pass the buzzard tree
The only birds- I ever see
In the buzzard tree
Are the buzzards
The other bird's fly by
They never seem to stop
In the buzzard tree
Maybe the buzzards
Are not friendly
Birds
I don't know why
But I never ever see
Any other birds
In that large large tree
Where the buzzards live,
In the tree- I call
The buzzard tree
I pass
Oh my way to work
Everyday.

Storms

Even in the storms of morning
The storms of noon, twilight, evening
A sun, a light shines thru
To guide as throes of despair
Chooses to darken the light given
Be anything- but dark, only dark.
And thru a guiding light
That shines thru all storms
Plus darkness
Faith of its choice is there for all
By choice- to make
And guides with its shimmering
Beautiful light
Once this choice is made
With guiding light
And most lovely, all the way
It's there
Guiding... thru the storms.
This light shines
Dimly- bright,
Beautiful...
Thru.

Water

If you plant
Your plants
Near water
They thrive better
Near the water
For their life, and...
You thrive best, near
The water.
Life is given
In the water
By the creator, of all
To the water
Plant your plants
Near the water
All thrives better
Near the water.

Race

A tricycle race
A tricycle race
They´re having a-
Tricycle race today,
Around, around, and around
They go-in a real,
Fun kind of way.
At the-children's
Tricycle race, tricycle race
The tricycle race
They´re having…
Today.

14

Chiba

Twas on the way
To chi-ba
In far off Japan
Of years, nearly...
Seventy or more,
Maybe so, ago.
I can remember
It plain- as seems
Part of a plan
A friend and I were
Told by a military member
Older that we to
Wait on the veranda
Of a home till others
Come by- and guide
Them on to chi- ba
Near by, with our jeep.
The lady in the home
Was nice to my friend
And I
Gave us some tea
And o- sem- bi
On which to dine
As we waited
To pass time by.
The day was nice
The weather too
Much time, has passed
Where my friend
The others too, are now
I'll never know
But will never forget.
Twas on the way
To chi-ba, that time
In far off Japan
Of years
Nearly seventy or more
Maybe so- of...
A long long time,
Ago.

A Beautiful Morning

Crystal blue were the skies above
Sending down
A special love
As the sun all golden
Set in the sky
Right beautiful
For an august
Summer eye
With a butter fly here
A bird over there
Moving- silent in the air...
And children- teachers
Other folks too
Inter viewing, talking, laughing
As most people
Always do.
On a lovely day in august
Under a crystal blue
Clear sky.
As, it- moved with the sun rays
Blended with love,
And started
A beautiful morning
A
Most
Lovely day.

Winter

The ways of winter
Are as bright sunshine
They glow in the shadows
And thru love they shine.
Like grass verdant green
The coldness it seems
To be...
As blossoms
Shimmering
Thru moonlight glow.
And the snows
Fill the mountains
And valleys
And fields
That green in the summers
Brief past.
Where their yield
In the harvest
Was beautiful full
Now the ways
Of the winter
Are beautiful too
For the harvest
Shines thru
Both summer and spring.
In a silence
That's beautiful
Yet love
Love... does ring
The ways oh...
The ways of winter.

Morning Sunshine

Hey there morning sunshine
Making each day
Your time
Kindly take me
With you
As you see the day
Thru
If I slip
Along the way.
Teach me too...
Spread love
Your way.
Always true
In what you do
Hey there morning sunshine
Kindly take me
With you.

Remain

A boy a girl
And a girl
And her friend
And the seagulls
With the clouds
And the sky, blue sky
In the still ness
Of the world
On a hill
Where forever
Flows silently beautiful by.
Will remain
Beautiful
And grow with memories
As the seasons
The children
Blue skies- flow by.

Curry and Rice

I do like
Chicken curry and rice
Especially
The way they make it
At an Oriental restaurant
A little eatery
In Castroville Ca…where
I like to go
They make it
Not to hot
But tasty too
And give you lots
And give you lots
And when you're thru
You feel real good
Its understood
Deep in your mind
You'll come back again
For more and more
I really do
Like
Chicken curry and rice
And... especially
They way- they make it there
Is,
Nice, real nice
And– tasty too.

Lovely Free

So lovely free
Are the birds that fly
In the wide open
Spacious sky.
They soar
High and low- these birds,
creating homes, families
Thru sunshine- thru storms
With faith- they move on.
For all Gods creations
Great or small
With faith- spiritual faith
Can create beauty
Beyond compare
And leave memories
Also love
Fulfilling love
That will travel
Silent as descending doves.
Or flow endless
On eternal rivers
Of...
The forever- soaring, soaring- free.

Circles

Semi circles - excessive
Television, gives
broken circles
families too.
Put folks back
in family circles.
Let the family - of
love...
Shine Thru.

The Ship

One evening the ship- with one,
I loved
Sailed quietly away
Not at full sail
But away.
To where the ocean
And the sky- meet as one
The ship- the ship
With one,
I loved aboard
Then disappeared from view
For me- to see
I, at that time, said to me
My love, my love
Is gone, forever
Gone from me.
Perhaps others far away
If the ship with my love
Sails in at full sail some day.
May say- here she comes. Here she comes
This I'll never know.
I only know-one evening
The ship with my love
Sailed quietly, away.

News

Bad news travels - like a bullet
getting round
Good new hardly...
ever gets to town.
But bad news, is like -
a storm coming in
and...
good news
Lets
The sunshine in

Special

We see the passing of the winter
as it turns - To blooms of spring
We see traces upon shorelines
where others lived
They there remain
visible is their history
As the worlds from where they came
And as spring a season beautiful soon to finish in its
way
Will show the traces
That finished on spring shorelines
washed with waves
as tides of life came thru
and summers arrived
Then Autumns, and of winters passing thru
to other springs
other seasons
for other reasons
That traces found upon the shorelines
were made with love
in that their season
and washed with waves
on life's ocean shore lines
to teach and reach
in a beautiful way
The passing thru of others
spiritually - with light - with love
misunderstood but... understood
a special given way
of other's special... given days
on this - our Earth.

So Nice

Tho I missed the interview
it was really
nice of you
To make the beautiful
Birthday Cards.
That brighten the days
in a wonderful way
with a love
That is present
as the glow
of the faraway stars,
and as near
as the breeze of spring
or sun beams are
Also... may each of you
have a beautiful day
That will extend
and extend and extend
as the winds
that travel
on and on and on
into - the...
forever.

Time Less

So beautiful
are the flowers of spring
which survive
without the need
of fret - or fear
for they are free - on the hillsides
spreading a certain
tremendous love
cared for
as the birds
that fly thru silence
above
Also things that slow
Tho painful
They may be- flow as ripples
of mountain streams
beautiful, clear, obscure
at times
as the flowers of spring
yet - all
constantly teaching love,
thru care
Lovely - Timeless
but forever
Like the flowers
Spring flowers
in silence
Do, timeless– beautiful.

Movin

Mr. Snail -
crawling on the ground
movin slow along
hardly makin a sound
Where are you going?
Hope you get there soon,
you can rest anytime
cause your house has room.

Pathways

As twilight gathered
mid the dusk of evening
Toward nightfall
and the ebbing sunlight rays
gleamed across
upon countryside.
With light
reflecting beauty
all around
from beauty of the universe
The evening
turned twilight
to night
and light
That reflected beauty
of the day
flowed with the
heavenly lights.
Creating beautiful memories
of the day, twilight,
evening, and night.
Of their
passing to rebirth
rebirth to passing
spiritually...
but living- on Eternally on.
on and on
in a beautiful way -
lighting heavenly pathways
in the forever - mid dusk of evening
toward nightfall.
Quietly, yet lovely.

The Way

Show me the way that the sands of time
drifts o'er the desert a far
And show me the way that the moon beams
align with the far off,
north star.
And tell me of the many many times
that the grains of the seashore sand
go and return and return again
leaving a shore... of beautiful sand.
Then there's the spider with broken web
That repairs it, again and again
To check an inner desire
That's part of a spiritual plan.
Or tell me of the ways of the trees
that have leaves
to fall and return - fall and return
and return with blossoms then leaves.
That flow with the seasons
Thru a beautiful fall
To a wondrous spring - admired by all.
As a butterfly from cocoon, rainbows
And storms give way
To bright sunshine, to light pathways
of spiritual light
That shine forever on
guiding showing the way
on the grains of sand
on the time
that we travel on
show me the way
please...
show me the way... of this.

Eternal

So gentle smooth
The surface of the ocean
hardly a wave can break
the tranquil scene
storms rush thru
short lived destructive
yet a healing light
guides bright
tho from afar
soft radiant
with love...
Spiritual and fulfilling
as- Tho with memories
of meaning
deep- within
for exquisitely beautiful,
forever
Eternal - The surface,
of the ocean's tranquil scene, returns
gentle smooth - as,
centuries pass lovely
Thru.

News

Bad news travels - like a bullet
getting round
Good new hardly...
ever gets to town.
But bad news, is like -
a storm coming in
and...
good news
Lets
The sunshine in.

Best

Maybe
you best don't do it
if you
don't feel good
about it
because
if you, don't feel good
about it
you won't feel good
if you do
maybe-you best-do it
if you do,
your way-for you.

Birthday party

A party, a party
A birthday party
A birthday party-for David
David's 5 years old, they say
He has a red hat on
Today.
Sitting in a chair
At the table
With children all around
Singing to the happy sound
Of happy birthday
David
Oh now... they're taking
A picture too
Of
A party, a party, a party
For David
He had a very,
Happy birthday party
And now...
Now its all thru
The party for David
David
Our, teddy bear.

Spookily Quiet

Oh so,
Spook-illy quiet
That's what it was
So quiet you could almost hear
A fly walk about
The wind was quiet
Leaves on trees were quiet
All was quiet
Even the most
Most
Of quiet ghosts
Were concerned
It was so quiet
Maybe
All noise
Had taken a vacation
A long, long vacation
And no one could scare anyone
For a long long time
That would be bad real bad
Everyone would be sad,
Real sad
It was so quiet-so...
Spook-illy quiet
That's what it was-twas so
A long long time ago.
Now...
All is ok
Noise...
Is
Here to stay.

Sunshine

You light up my life
A special way
Like sunshine does
When it shines
Each day
Then the days they fly
Good thoughts
Pass by
When I think of you
Or I even try.
You light my life
You light up my life
A special way
Every day-every day.
Every...single day.

Water

If you plant
Your plants
Near water
They thrive better
Near the water
For their life, and...
You thrive best, near
The water.
Life is given
In the water
By the creator, of all
To the water
Plant your plants
Near the water
All thrives better
Near the water.

A Sailing Ship

One evening-a ship
It sailed from the port
To far, far away
Thru the waters of the ocean
Thru its waves
Right before twilight of evening
Right before close of day
Till the ship-a sailing ship
Sailed with sails
Of white, at full
To a mere speck in the waves
To where the sky meets the sea
At the horizon.
The ship sailed on- forever on
At full sail
Fading, gradually, finally
Wonderfully, beautifully
As day light that
Leaves the sky
After
A lovely, lovely
Sunset.
The ship sailed- it sailed
From view
From port
To the far...
Far away.

Old Friends

Finding looking up
Old friends
Of long age
Is like finding
Snow, from winter
In summer
Now, just where
Did it go?
Unless, its like ice
A little of
What it was long ago.
But if its water
Its easy to scatter
So its hard
To know.
Finding old friends
From long age
Its hard to know
Just where to go- Cause
Seems old friends, go.

23

Buzzard tree

Oh my way to work
Everyday
I pass the buzzard tree
The only birds- I ever see
In the buzzard tree
Are the buzzards
The other bird's fly by
They never seem to stop
In the buzzard tree
Maybe the buzzards
Are not friendly
Birds
I don't know why
But i never ever see
Any other birds
In that large large tree
Where the buzzards live,
In the tree- I call
The buzzard tree
I pass
Oh my way to work
Everyday.

Storms

Even in the storms of morning
The storms of noon, twilight, evening
A sun, a light shines thru
To guide as throes of despair
Chooses to darken the light given
Be anything- but dark, only dark.
And thru a guiding light
That shines thru all storms
Plus dark ness
Faith of its choice is there for all
By choice- to make
And guides with its shimmering
Beautiful light
Once this choice is made
With guiding light
And most lovely, all the way
It's there
Guiding... thru the storms.
This light shines
Dimly- bright,
Beautiful...
Thru.

Of Night

In the late of night
When its nearly morning
Its just as quiet
As quiet can almost be
For it seems
All is quiet
Except some noise...darkness,
Which can't sleep
Quietly
In the late of night
When its just as quiet
As quiet
Can almost...
Be.

Bumps

Troubles
they're only
bumps
in the road
they must be -
the rest
of the road,
is smooth
as can be.

Chiba

Twas on the way
To chi-ba
In far off Japan
Of years, nearly...
Seventy or more,
Maybe so, ago.
I can remember
It plain- as seems
Part of a plan
A friend and I were
Told by a military member
Older that we to
Wait on the veranda
Of a home till others
Come by- and guide
Them on to chi- ba
Near by, with our jeep.
The lady in the home
Was nice to my friend
And I
Gave us some tea
And o- sem- bi
On which to dine
As we waited
To pass time by.
The day was nice
The weather too
Much time, has passed
Where my friend
The others too, are now
I'll never know
But will never forget.
Twas on the way
To chi-ba, that time
In far off japan
Of years
Nearly seventy or more
Maybe so- of...
A long long time,
Ago.

A Beautiful Morning

Crystal blue were the skies above
Sending down
A special love
As the sun all golden
Set in the sky
Right beautiful
For an august
Summer eye
With a butter fly here
A bird over there
Moving- silent in the air...
And children- teachers
Other folks too
Inter viewing, talking, laughing
As most people
Always do.
On a lovely day in august
Under a crystal blue
Clear sky.
As, it- moved with the sun rays
Blended with love,
And started
A beautiful morning
A
Most
Lovely day.

Circles

Semi circles - excessive
Television, gives
broken circles
families too.
Put folks back
in family circles.
Let the family - of
love...
Shine Thru.

Morning Sunshine

Hey there morning sunshine
Making each day
Your time
Kindly take me
With you
As you see the day
Thru
If I slip
Along the way.
Teach me too...
Spread love
Your way.
Always true
In what you do
Hey there morning sunshine
Kiudly take me
With you.

Soon

Eat tomatoes pie
Watch an elephant fly
See an alligator ride
A bicycle by
And watch the sun
Up high
Then while it sets
Low in the sky.
To stand.
And say...
I've had a nice day
My friend,
Seen some of
The very best
Today-I have,
Have I.

Wide Range

Isn't life strange
Life covers a wide, wide, range
Those we thought- not our friends
Become friends thru ways
Of strange.
Even thru war at times
Later
Strangers become family lifetime friends
With love- true love...
Have families, sometime,
Lots of time.
Love each others countries
For lifetimes- lifetimes, after
Isn't life strange...
Life covers a wide, wide, range.

Light

The mornings are beautiful
For they come in a way
As light from above
And flowers of love
That flows soft
On pillars of light
And awakens the world
A special way
From dark- to the light of day.
Meaningful- beautiful
Comforting and silently
As a river flows
Memorably on.
Beautiful as from the start
Like light from above
With care...
With love.
The mornings are beautiful.

There's Today

Way past the sea
Up next to the sky
Where soft the hours
Just drift- slow by
And the sky is crystal blue
Reflecting quiet
With beauty thru
To each day- especially today
Cause...
Soft the hours- just drift today
As the heavens
Send love
In most beautiful
Lovely ways
Look... yes look
Way past the sea
Up next to the sky
And...
Theres today.

Lovely Free

So lovely free
Are the birds that fly
In the wide open
Spacious sky.
They soar
High and low- these birds,
creating homes, families
Thru sunshine- thru storms
With faith- they move on.
For all Gods creations
Great or small
With faith- spiritual faith
Can create beauty
Beyond compare
And leave memories
Also love
Fulfilling love
That will travel
Silent as descending doves.
Or flow endless
On eternal rivers
Of...
The forever- soaring, soaring- free.

Remain

A boy a girl
And a girl
And her friend
And the seagulls
With the clouds
And the sky, blue sky
In the still ness
Of the world
On a hill
Where forever
Flows silently beautiful by.
Will remain
Beautiful
And grow with memories
As the seasons
The children
Blue skies- flow by.

The Ship

One evening the ship- with one,
I loved
Sailed quietly away
Not at full sail
But away.
To where the ocean
And the sky- meet as one
The ship- the ship
With one,
I loved aboard
Then disappeared from view
For me- to see
I, at that time, said to me
My love, my love
Is gone, forever
Gone from me.
Perhaps others far away
If the ship with my love
Sails in at full sail some day.
May say- here she comes. Here she comes
This I'll never know.
I only know-one evening
The ship with my love
Sailed quietly, away.

Special

We see the passing of the winter
as it turns - To blooms of spring
We see traces upon shorelines
where others lived
They there remain
visible is their history
As the worlds from where they came
And as spring a season beautiful soon to finish in its
way
Will show the traces
That finished on spring shorelines
washed with waves
as tides of life came thru
and summers arrived
Then Autumns, and of winters passing thru
to other springs
other seasons
for other reasons
That traces found upon the shorelines
were made with love
in that their season
and washed with waves
on lifes ocean shore lines
to teach and reach
in a beautiful way
The passing thru of others
spiritually - with light - with love
misunderstood but... understood
a special given way
of other's special... given days
on this - our Earth.

So Nice

Tho I missed the interview
it was really
nice of you
To make the beautiful
Birthday Cards.
That brighten the days
in a wonderful way
with a love
That is present
as the glow
of the faraway stars,
and as near
as the breeze of spring
or sun beams are
Also... may each of you
have a beautiful day
That will extend
and extend and extend
as the winds
that travel
on and on and on
into - the...
forever.

Pathways

As twilight gathered
mid the dusk of evening
Toward nightfall
and the ebbing sunlight rays
gleamed across
upon countryside.
With light
reflecting beauty
all around
from beauty of the universe
The evening
turned twilight
to night
and light
That reflected beauty
of the day
flowed with the
heavenly lights.
Creating beautiful memories
of the day, twilight,
evening, and night.
Of their
passing to rebirth
rebirth to passing
spiritually...
but living- on Eternally on.
on and on
in a beautiful way -
lighting heavenly pathways
in the forever - mid dusk of evening
toward nightfall.

The Way

Show me the way that the sands of time
drifts o'er the desert a far
And show me the way that the moon beams
align with the far off,
north star.
And tell me of the many many times
that the grains of the seashore sand
go and return and return again
leaving a shore... of beautiful sand.
Then there's the spider with broken web
That repairs it, again and again
To check an inner desire
That's part of a spiritual plan.
Or tell me of the ways of the trees
that have leaves
to fall and return - fall and return
and return with blossoms then leaves.
That flow with the seasons
Thru a beautiful fall
To a wondrous spring - admired by all.
As a butterfly from cocoon, rainbows
And storms give way
To bright sunshine, to light pathways
of spiritual light
That shine forever on
guiding showing the way
on the grains of sand
on the time
that we travel on
show me the way
please...
show me the way... of this.

Eternal

So gentle smooth
The surface of the ocean
hardly a wave can break
the tranquil scene
storms rush thru
short lived destructive
yet a healing light
guides bright
tho from afar
soft radiant
with love...
Spiritual and fulfilling
as- Tho with memories
of meaning
deep- within
for exquisitely beautiful,
forever
Eternal- The surface,
of the ocean's tranquil scene, returns
gentle smooth - as,
centuries pass lovely
Thru.

Easy

Puzzles are
difficult
easy too
if you know
just what
to do.

Shade

The shade was there
when
the tree was there
they
cut the tree
down
now there's no shade
there
maybe the tree
took the shade
when
the tree went away
cause there's
no shade there
today
and...
the shade was there
when
the tree was there
where is the shade?

The Moon

I seen the moon
in the sky
high in the sky
right before
the sunset too
maybe the moon
wanted to see
all it could see
before dark
came thru-
and use sunlight
for free.
Maybe...
because -
I seen the moon
quite high in the sky
before sunset
and...
I told the moon
Hi.

An Apple

Cut and apple
in half
follow the right
path
there is a little star
and in the star
there are seeds
that will grow
an apple tree
with apples to eat
for you - and yes
for me.
If you,
cut an apple
in half
and -
follow the right
path
there is a little star
with seeds.

A Holiday

A day to relax
sleep late too
eat, run,
go for a picnic
do most anything
good
you want to do
is
A holiday
for everyone
and you
a day all relax
and enjoy too.

Weather

The wind is blowing
The sun is shining
The sky is blue
clouds not many
only a few
its cool today
with weather
to like - for you
if you do
and the wind
and the sun
also the sky
is blue - crystal blue
for you...
Too.

To Fly

Today just passed
right by
it seemed to fly.
My my how it
just flew
it was morning
it was noon
then night time
too
today just passed
right by
my, my how it.
Just flew,
of course...
It's supposed to
so night time
can come
thru.

Company

If you are
alone
in the moonlight
with
none other
to keep you company.
You and
the moonlight alone
keep each other
company.

Protect

There was a day
some went away
to protect
the life we love
did they
some come back
some their lives
there
they left
did they
we honor all those
that went away
that day
on veterans
day.

Collection

A collage
is a collection
of very important
items -good for memories
glued to a piece
of paper
card board or something
of size picked for the
items
by the artist-usually
about 3-4-5 maybe
6 yrs. of age
and made
especially for mom-dad
or
loved ones-with love.
when the artist
is carefully-painstakingly
finished
with much thought
and love
drew their name-any where
on the page
as with age the very best
they could.
the collage the collection
of important items
is given with...
admiration and
appreciation...too-to loved ones.
when the
artist
is, thru.

Angels

Angels are here
they're there
they are every where
they help you thru
they help you thru
they look at you
seldom speak to you
and then they go
to help others thru.
Angels are here
they're there
they are
every where.

Roars

The quiet
is quiet
in the day
the quiet
is quiet
in the night
and only roars
when we disturb
it
and then
again
the quiet
is quiet.

Star

In the very center
of every apple
there is a little star
and in this star
there are seeds
that will grow
an apple tree
with apples
to eat
for you, and yes
for me
in the very center
of every
every apple.

A Special Day

Cool the weather
November's here
sometime the patter
of rain I hear
also-someday
sunshine's bright
a sky of blue
of autumn
passes thru
with crisp of leaves
full harvest moon
all silvery bright
and cool
the brisk of nights
then...just before
November leaves-to say
"hello" December
it brings,
thanksgiving day
a special day-that comes
in just
November.

In The Sky

There's an airplane
in the sky
I hear an airplane
flying by
I wonder
where the airplane
in the sky
is going
flying by.

Spent

Eternity
spent
where the heart
is free
would maybe
be spent
as clouds drift
high in a crystal
blue sky
just eternally happy
and free.

Guidance

Wisdom
lovely is wisdom
beautiful too
it brings the most
in all we do.
By giving good
guidance
as stars are above
have since creation,
from wisdom
thru love.

Sunday

Sunday seems
kinda like
a different day
in a way
from other days
seems like most folks
think so too
and kind of
treat Sunday
different
cause
Sunday seems
kinda special
its way.

A Special Day

Cool the weather
November's here
sometime the patter
of rain I hear
also-somedays
sunshine's bright
a sky of blue
of autumn
passes thru
with crisp of leaves
full harvest moon
all silvery bright
and cool
the brisk of nights
then...just before
November leaves-to say
"hello" December
it brings,
thanks giving day
a special day-that comes
in just
November.

Said

Baa, baa-said the sheep
Moo-moo-said the cow
Neigh-neigh-said the horse
Oink-oink-said the pig
Ribbit-ribbit-said the frog
Meow-meow-said the cat
and the rat said
quiet...cat.

Invite

If a ghost-came over
and sat by you
today
what would you
to the ghost
say
would you hold
the ghost hand
and-say to the ghost
lets go get
a pizza
and some
popcorn too
the ghost might
like you
to say that too
and if you did
the ghost might
go with you
and say
thank you, then
invite you
to a visit
with the ghost
at the
ghost house
a real, real
ghost house
try it do it
too
If a ghost
comes and
sits with you
anytime
any day.
I dare you to,
this do.

Water Table

There's boats
in the table
there's fish
in the table
there's water in the table
a hippopotamus
and an alligator too
put there
by children.
Take a look
at the boats
and everything
in the, water table
zoo.

A Calm

Play some music
and in its way
send by
ear
to soul
calm
in music's way.
and if-you play
the music
too
music speaks
its way-
to you.

A Mask

Make a mask
of yesterday
then
today
can feel
can be
some of
yesterday.

Cat

I locked my long haired
black cat
in the garage
on Halloween night
because...
witches ride brooms
with black cats too
hollering-hee,hee,hee
boo-ooo-ooo-ooo
who-ooo-ooo-ooo
and off they go
toward the moon
I don't want her the witch to take
my cat too,
so I locked my long haired black
cat in the garage.
Wouldn't you do that
too.

Halloween

On that special day
when evening came
all the children then
they came
with their bags-and
costumes too
ringing door bells,
saying
trick or treat
and we thank you
then off and
down the street
they go in...the street light glow
on that special, special day
of
Halloween.

Strange

Love, strange is love
true love
tho silent it be
for one to find
another too
tho few, tho thousands be
tho miles away at times
when comes the day
true love-will find the,
right place-right time
communication-meeting too
for years, family
thru...love yet
strange is love
true, silent is
love.

Reminders

Shadows left on the ground
in a picture
there they stay
of the house-long since gone
where...
I was born,
in the picture-there it stays.
Shadows in a picture
of my sister-and an old tree
where she stood
near an old church buildings
all long,long gone away
to stay.
In the picture tho
there the shadow stays,
shadow of my sister and all
there it stays.
Shadow in a picture near the
roof line of an old school
building where I attended
kindergarten 75 years ago
in the picture
there it stays.
tho the buildings ,gone
years ago away.
Shadows-shadows do that
in a picture there they stay.
They're memories
too
they stay
in
and with
the picture, that
they, do.

The Dawn

Right before the dawn
sets in
in early, early
morning
it usually gets quiet
quiet as can be
I guess that's when
the ghosts-of
late, late night
are resting.
for it gets
quiet as can be-to me
right before the dawn
sets in
in early, early
morning.

Less

With less
big
pres-en-ta-shuns
little
e-lab-bor-ra-shuns
say what
there is to say
and be with
haste...
Back on the
wide,
high way.

Child Hood

Its fun to do
as a child
we've done
some things we do
all, life time thru.
for in each one, perhaps
a child's life stays
that is awakened
by what we do
on
Some days.
The thing's of
Child hood days.

Hazy

Sky
of blue,
clouds cover today
the sunshine too
is hazy.
An airplane
tho
high over the clouds
I hear it
flying by.
It must see
the sky of blue
and sunshine too
above it,
where under a sky of blue
over the clouds it be
and for miles
clear, can see.
While we below
the clouds
today
only
hazy, see.

A Scene

Flowers of purple
both dark and light
with leaves of green– growing,
on a fence of wood
produce imaginative
valleys and meadows
that fully cover
most of the fence
of wood
giving a beautiful
scene.
Of-imaginative
valleys and meadows
of flowing flowers
of purple-leaves of green
on a fence of wood
this…gives
To view,
A, rather-beautiful scene-and children
it seems, love it.

Late

Sleep
too
late
work
late
too.

Along

With the sun
arise
and exercise
move along
with the sun thru-out
the day
repose-with
the sun
and moon
stars of night
arise with
the sun
continue-continue
follow
the sun moon
the stars
follow their guide
faith full
they are
there they-will be
thru-out
eternity
forever-forever
forever
and on, for you.

Consume

A stationary bicycle
and tread mill too
I use to help
consume the edibles
I use.
That tread mill
is nearly new
the bicycles old
their value
a point of view
each day old
each day new
as I continue
continue
continue
to eat
and use,
the stationary bicycles
and
tread mill too
their value tho of exercise
"most" to be
true.

The Ball

Bounce the ball
throw the ball
thru a hoop
wait its fall
pick it up
throw it far
people holler
he's a star
throw the ball
bounce the ball
basket ball
basket ball
basket ball.

A Hug

No body ever
gives me a hug any more
I know I'm almost ninety
just a little hug
don't matter how tiny,
a little hug would do.
Real tight until its thru
cause...
No body gives me a hug,
anymore.

Sleep

Music, music
played
late at night
soothes
the soul
with music's delight
and causes
sleep
to come-and stay
till late
the hour
of coming
day.

Hot

Its warm today
the weathers hot
and cool today
then weather's not
the sky is blue
the grass is green
there are no clouds
none to be seen
the moon at night
it does come out
but in the day
its not about
there are no clouds
the sky is blue
today is warm
the weather's hot.

Gardens

Children and snails
and gardens too
kind of go together
and when they do
children pick up
snails
and kind of
wonder to
why snails do
just what they do.
When they do.
and snails probably
wonder to
what children do
and
why they do
what they do
children and snails
and gardens too
kind of go together
when they do.

Flying By

Little white airplane
flying by
I see you flying
high in the sky
with fleecy white
clouds
drifting by
little white airplane
flying by
where are you going?
singing, so happy
in the sky.

Horses

The horses
the horses
the horses
the horses are running
by
they're stick horses
with children
they're shouting
they're playing
and having fun too
and that's ok
until they're thru
cause-we
like to hear
so near
the horses
the horses
the horses
the horses running
the stick horses
with children
shouting
and
playing
just having fun to
let them run
run, run, run
until they're thru.

The Beach

Off to the beach
the girls did go
pushing the wagons
as they go
taking their dolls
doll blankets too
baskets to carry
the dolls
went too
the boys were watching
maybe the girls
wanted them to.
The beach the beach
but theres no water here
when you're 4 or 5
no one really cares
the beach can be
most anywhere.
And off to the beach
the girls did go
pushing their wagons
as they go.
and the boys-the boys
went too

Each Day

So strange
each day
its moments,
brew.
So strange
each day-a book
its meaning
gives
to you.

Fear

Thinking
imagination
creation
fear
Visualization
clouds
hazy-reality
Sunshine-while thinking.

Another Day

Take that building
That's been knocked down
piled in piles
all around and
put it in places
back on earth
to be used
another day
to build on earth
again
as something
planned for use
another way.

Tonight

Its so quiet tonight
that when the wind
blows-it seems
to know, it is
to blow real, quiet
so the leaves
move real, slow
kind of la-zy like.
The wind seems
to know
the wind seems
to know
because...
Its so quiet
tonight.

You

Miss
too much
sleep
soon...not
too much
you.

History

A moment in history
when all
listen to the story
at hand
what ever the story
in history
maybe in the land
if it concerns many
as never before
and if the problem
is new-to hear-to see
for you and for me
that moment, in history
will be listened to
by all
and the concern-will be
interesting to see
of that moment
maybe -it is
a moment in history that
will be, there.
to see-to see
to see.

The Pumpkins

When the pumpkins
all big and orange
and round
when it snows
and the moon is pretty
and its full-and round
old jack frost, gets
weather cool
then the frost sets in
and the leaves
turn brown, golden brown
start to fall, fall
just-drift down
and the vines get dry
they start to snap
the harvest moon, shines high
with the stars
tho seems, not too high
in the sky
the birds all fly
way south in the sky
then snow soon falls
soft, soft, soft
so soft from the sky
covering the ground
with a blanket
of pretty snow white
cause thats the time
thats just, just right
where it snows
when the pumpkins
all big and orange
and round
when the pumpkins
the pumpkins
when the pumpkins...
Come to town.

Cat

The cat woman
the cat woman
all the cats know...
The cat woman too
and
they wave their tails
say meow, meow, meow
when she goes
thru
all the cats
small cats
big cats
medium too
all the cats
know the cat woman
when she goes thru
she drives
a big, big car
goes fast, slow, too
and says
meow, meow, meow
how are you
the cat woman
the cat woman
is here with you
all the cats
know
the cat woman
the cat woman
all...
The cats do.

Hop Scotch

Come play
hop scotch
jump with me
hop on one foot
one-two-three
two feet down
hop on one foot
two feet down
one more
then
one foot down
two feet down
and then with
the hop scotch
you're go thru-again
and again
as you want to
come play
hop scotch
jump with me
hop scotch is
great fun
you'll see.

So Nice

The weather is
so nice today
with sky of blue
and sunshine too
a little wind
that stirs-the leaves
on-our
one tree
and...
I seen one bird
just fly-slow by
everything
seems   slow
with out
much go
because
the weather
is so nice
today.

Stew

I see a little girl
in the sand box
near
mixing sand
with water too
making-I-think
a mud stew
no one else-I see
has mud stew
in the sand box here.
If this sand box sand
makes good mud stew
this little girl
with
this sand box sand
made very very good
sand box
stew.

45

Experienced

Unless others
Have experienced
How it feels to
See, feel and be
After the young
Have grown and left
And you lose your
Spouse
The creators special way
You are alone day to day
Unless others have experiences
The same they feel, see, be
No need to tell them
How you feel at times
They never understand
They cannot feel be
As you then do.
After the years
Time together have…
Flowed thru
For each glows in their own light
Much as sunlight
Moonlight
Differ with light.
Beautiful tho each
Their own way
And others feel too– their way
As life's like crystal mountain
Streams flow,
Magnificently on.

Thru Fog

People on the shore line
viewed in fog
from far away
appear as
people
walking robots
viewed thru
fog
in the far
away.

The Skyline

Where the ocean
meets the sky line
in the far, far, far away
is as smooth
and straight
as a line
can be
and will always
always
be
that way.

Hoboes

Drift wood
from the ocean
hoboes...
and
riders of the
ocean waves
for free.
From where ever,
their homes
May be.

Never Ending

Waves, waves, waves
ocean waves
crashing, crashing, crashing
on shorelines
wondrously, beautifully
never ending
most lovely
thunderously
quietly-speaking
to whom to whom
to whom?
To whom ever
comes
under standing ,,,
to them
the waves.
Speak
quietly
thunderously
wonderfully, beautifully
crashing, crashing, crashing
never ending...
on shore lines.

Crows

I seen a flock
of many crows
today
and they did fly
to trees
of
about three
did they
and then
to a farmers field
did fly
and checked the
field for
something good
of taste
they know
was there
a party
they the crows
appeared to have
in mind
and in this field
perhaps
for these crows
the party
all prepared
for them
this party
there
they planned
to find
and they were going
in a group
to not be late
for this party date
when I seen
the flock
of crows
today
and they did fly
to this field
as I was driving
passing
by.

Hair

The children
wonder
at gray
of hair
and-seem
to accept
for all
somewhere, in time
it comes
there.

Graceful

Two seagulls
now
they just flew
by
so graceful-and quiet
were they
in the clear
blue sky.
They seemed
a part
of
the crystal
blue sky.

Places

Wheels of round
and
axles too
gets
us around
and
takes us
to
places
where-we
should
and sometime
should not.
Even
be
going to.
wheels and axles
too
sometime
do.

The Quiet

When its
quiet
and even
movement
of an
ant
seems that
of
thunder
music-music
lovely
can change
the quiet
to love
and beautiful
wonder
as it flows
the quiet...
thru.

Quietly

Help and help
quietly
where help
is
needed
if
you do
light of love
lovely
shines thru.
Seen lovely quietly too.

The Pilot

The pilot of an airplane
sees then world in a way
that's different from
how its seen from
most other ways.
For its
low its high its slow
its fast its above the clouds
next to blue in the sky
with no trees, or anything
but wide open sky.
Then to come back to earth
after flight in the sky
one appreciates the daily flight life
of a bird
small, large
ascending, descending
the sky.
The sky-the sky
oh the beautiful sky
the pilot of an airplane
sees the world in a way
quite different
from others
as we. Travel the world
while it-slowly swirls
its way-day to day.

Me and the World

When the world
don't seem
to like me
I try to meet
the world
at least
half way
and when the world
likes me
I drag in the
other half.
Then the pieces
the world and I
walk together
pretty good
for a pretty long way
till the world
don't seem to like me
again
sometime…Tho
I don't like me
too so
guess I can't
altogether
blame the world, maybe its-
me and the world.

Thank You

Oh say
could you afford
to give me
a hug?
Its very cheap
in its way.
And you really
won't miss
a hug.
If you honestly
freely
give it away.
And…
Thank you.

The Sound

I heard the sound
of foot steps
and then
they went away
but twas only
the wind just blowing
in its windy kind of way.
I heard the sound
of voices
and twas children
playing near.
I heard the sound
of quiet
and it stayed
forever near
the way one hears
the sound you hear
kind of makes
you believe
the sound you hear
is near.

The

Humming birds
the colors-of the
humming birds
are so beautiful
to see
as they zip
and fly
all around us
so very
rapidly
few other birds
can compare
to the beautiful
wee small
humming bird
zipping, zipping
flying...
oh, so swiftly...
in the air.

When

When you're in
the quiet
with just quiet
all around
for a long, long time
no other sound
just...
Take a deep breath
a real deep breath
and say
who-oo-whoo-oo
whoo-oo
the quiet will
answer you
and you then
ask the quiet
hey quiet
hey quiet
Who is you?
If the quiet answers
run
make quick foot sounds.
When you're in the quiet
with just quiet
all around.

Cat

Old cat
layin in the yard
sleepin and a lis-nin
and a watchin too
everything...
Walkin or a slippin
or just
passin thru.

Visit

Whales
are so big
and frogs
so small
whales
never visit
frog-homes
at all.

Talk

Rabbits
never talk
I never
heard them
they go
almost-every where
for-every where
almost
you see them
yet...
I never heard
a rabbit
talk,
have you
ever
heard them?.
talk.

Like Butterflies

If you could fly
like butter flies fly
you could go
where butter flies go
you could fly with
birds and bees
you could fly
where wind blows leaves
on trees
you could fly
here and there
and almost
any where
real-real quiet
in the air
butter flies
sometime fly
far far away
you could do this too
if you could fly
like butter flies do
if you really
wanted to.
You could fly
for hours and hours
flying in meadows
of beautiful flowers
if you could fly
like butter flies do
If you really...
Wanted to.

Things to do

Many things to do
all
at one time too
can confuse you
or most
any one
so
slow down, slow down
and
think things
thru
then
do,
cause...
Many things to do
all
at one time too
can make,
an almost
stranger
out of you.

Loved

When the ones
you loved
have gone
and
you feel that they
are here
they are here with you
in a special way
and you
only you know
and feel
that special way
its true-its true to you
when the ones you loved
have gone
they can visit with you
a special way and you understand
that special time
that special day.

Halloween Night

Ghosts and goblins
come out soon
underneath a
harvest moon
they travel light
and in the night
dressed up scary
dressed up light
they like candy
hand outs
too
come on
Halloween nights
knock on doors
saying
trick or treat
and boo
with bags to fill
and a big
thank you
then
on and on
from house to house
they go.
Ghosts and goblins
come out soon
underneath a
harvest moon
and in...
The
street light,
glow.

52

To Catch

They are trying
to catch
a butter fly
it flies so quiet in the sky
sometime
by them...
It flies right by
they are trying
to catch
a butter fly
maybe it sees
them too
maybe the butter fly
don't want
them too.
they are trying to catch
a butter fly
now they are all
just going away
they all wanted
to catch
a butter fly
maybe they
will try again
another day
butter flies
are so
beautiful
and quiet
in the sky
I think
we should all
just admire
then
and let then
fly.
How about you
do you like butter flies
do you catch butter flies
butter flies
are beautiful
in the sky.

Work

Clocks and watches
work so hard
they tell us
when to start
they tell us
when to stop
they tell us
when to go
to work
they tell us
when to go
back home
they tell us
when its time
for school
and when to
go home too.
They tell us
when to go
to bed
and when to
get up too
clocks and watches
tell us
when its time
to do most
everything
we do
clocks and watches
work so hard
they really
really do.

Halfway

continues ...halfway

Stuck halfway
between a dream-and awake
was I
and it seemed-so real
it was, scary too-scary too
I could see-a lot
for in the dark
I was
camping
in the forest-I was-I was
and it was so strange
it felt so strange
it did-it did
stuck halfway
between a dream-and awake
as I was-I was
I remembered a
flash light
that I had-I had
turned it on
and looked around-all around
all around
to fully awake me
back to reality-to reality
from being stuck halfway-stuck halfway
between a dream-a dream
and awake-and awake
that I was having-was having
where the people-the people
and the light I seen
reflecting on them-on them
I could see
sleeping
camping
where I was

all so real-all so real
I never will forget
that dream
and what it done
for me to see-me to see
flashing light as if
thru parted window blinds
for me to see-on folks
stuck halfway between a dream-a dream
and reality
as was I-as was I
and this is true-is true
could happen to you-to you
if you are ever
stuck halfway
between a dream and awake
and reality- and reality.

continued

54

Gently

A little wind
to make the clouds drift
slow, slow thru
and sky blue peeks...
soft soft thru
another beautiful day
is passing-just... passing
hazy, hazy, thru
with...a little wind
a hammer
I don't -see it
but I hear it
some body's hammering
hammering, hammering, hammering
hitting, hitting
with, a hammer, a hammer
its relaxing too
tools do that to you
they do
I don't see it
but, I hear it
some body hammering
hitting, hitting, hitting
with a hammer, a hammer
and they're doing something
not too far away
gently, gently
like
a little wind
makes the clouds
drift
slow, slow, thru
all this together
helps another day flow
just lovely, lovely
thru.

Walking

I was walking
in a park one day
I seen a little
ground squirrel
the squirrel stopped
and looked at me
seemed to say
"hey you"
why are you
looking at me
that way
this is my home
you stay away
then the ground squirrel
went in his hole
and away
feeling good that day
I walked on by
the ground squirrels home
on my way
as I was walking
in the park
that day.

This Real

Camping near the ocean
was I
maybe 1 or 2 weeks ago.
Watched the ocean waves
arriving, leaving
I know that they had traveled
witnessed much.
As they came and went
touching the shore
leaving waves of memory
gathered from afar
and memories are
lovely, beautiful
spiritual too
as they come to us with love.
While we camp briefly
In this realm,
passing thru.

Happiness

Three little birds
I see
just hopping hopping
quite happily
hopping all around
taking turns
eating something
they found
lying on the ground
some food-some one
threw away
three little birds
I see-very happy
today
eating-eating something
some one
threw away
some one made
some birds
very happy today
three birds-I see
and they didn't know
because...
Happiness comes
in quiet ways.

The Way

A compass helps
to find
the way
but read
the compass
correctly
what ever-your compass may be.
Night or day
then
go carefully
all the way.
Sometimes
even then
things move
and its hard
the way
but...
A compass helps.

For You

That book has
pictures
of forever
in it
for you
for most others
maybe no
but for you
those pictures, the book
you
and memory
know forever.
That book has
pictures
of forever
in it
for you.

Carrying

Now one-before two
two as many
one few
lonesome too.
Fears with honesty
subside
as dark-with light
cannot reside.
One-left ones
tomorrow too
your tomorrow
that-now
is new
use tomorrow
build a new.
Look the world, right
in the eye
mix
grief with honesty
they both, will fly
some at a time
will much less-that be
to carry thru
and-that helps too.
Cry some too-for when
you do
much seems to look
different
thru eyes, that do
do-what you must
work your way thru
hammer things pound
write paint whatever
do in your way
all helps
you
on the way
day by day
friends help much
with special touch
as talking, listen, quiet
much like

continued

twilight, evening, moonlight
dawn...
soaking thru.
Food-work-honesty all
help quietly in their way
as one steps
three steps forward
and one step back
for years at times
carrying the one
that left
forever-with love
in love
connecting-silently
with and one's
heart...
Thru-day
and...
day by day.

Everyone

Help others
help others
help your own self too
then...
Every one,
can make it thru.

Emotions

That which makes
us what we are
like the moon
high up-up with
the stars.
In the lovely
love
that was given-that
and
our emotions
given
by our creation.
Makes us
what we are
like the moon
high up-up with
the stars.
Helps
make the heavens

A Blanket

The covering cover
of a blanket
over those in need
placed by those, who care
silently…
and thru love.
Can be a symbol
of love unfolding
like sky blue-in the heaven
above.
By those who view
silently-in distance
and unseen
this caring cover
placed thru care
by those who care
deeply-for others
and...
Thru love.
a blanket- the cover of a blanket, of love.

Only One

When you're one
in the house
everything you do
is only you
it involves only you
what you eat...and
everything, everything
you do.
Not like
when there were two
doing all together
as before.
you have to now
think,
just what did I do
today
when I done this-or that
today, and how
now
that you're-the only
one
in the house.

Alone

A wolf-when
its all alone
will bark
at the moon
in its tone
and a person
for
a person's
an animal
will do the same
it will sing
to the moon the quiet
it self or
any thing.
When its lonesome.
So will you
when your time comes.
to.

Rest

Why don't you stop
and take some
time off to rest?
Oh no, the world
might stop
if I do.
You're wrong my friend
your world-will rest
if you do.
You know...
I think you're right
I'll take a rest
that way both world's
the real world-mine too
can better
get thru.

Storms

When storms comes
of this
of storms
we know
storms will never ever
forever
in one place be
storms pass as ships
on the endless sea
their tracks forever lost
that be.
When storms come
they pass...
of storms
this,
we know.
So
stay the course.
See them thru.

Visitor

Being a visitor in this world
for less that 100 years
more for a few
who wish they know.
Less for some
all never know
what should one do.
To really really
float right thru
being a visitor here
for most
more or less
for...100 years.

Constructively

Blood, blood
spilled by others
to get for
others
what others wants
from others
by wars
there must be
better ways
to spend
the 100 years
more or less
visiting here
than spilling blood, blood
but by using
blood
constructively.

Away

Fossil fuel
fossil fuel
when its no more
how ya gonna
run
the store
solar power
might
slowly
help in
a way
cause its here
some where
every single day.
Fossil fuel-fossil fuel
may someday
slip slowly
away.

Scary

Ghosts are scary
so I'm told
and that they never
ever do grow old.
That someone
can always see them
where-ever they be
this may or may not be
but if it is
then...
True twill be.
And-we'll know
ghosts are scary
that they never
ever do grow old
and that someone
ghosts can see
where-ever
they.
May ever
be.

Lost

Lost, lost, lost
in a sea
of no one
you know to be.
Found, found, found
in a world
of no one
you know to see.
Then-by
viewing deep
inside
where the lost
you really
resides
you found you
the lost you
you found...
You.

Try

No job
try try
while the world
goes by
to old
to hire
to young
to retire
what to do
to just
get thru
having
no job
while the world
goes by
just,
try try
try try.

Holds

The bottom
holds the middle
the middle
holds the top.
If the bottom slips
the middle moves
the top does too
it shivers, shimmeys, shakes.
If
help don't come
and soon
to help the top do
what its supposed
to do.
Stay where its
supposed to stay
when
the bottom slips
and middle moves
shimmeys
shakes
starts to kinda
turning
round and round
everything
soon falls
down
down-to the
ground.
So keep tryin do it right.

Locust

When hordes
of locust
focus
on fields of green
fields of green
are soon
unseen
when locust focus.

Nature

What we have done
accomplished and
can do
the powers of nature
it seems
when unleashed
like a hurricane
can easily
completely
literally
un do.
Also even using most materials
and methods we rebuild
with, the powers of nature
plays with
as toys-and quickly
very quickly, destroys.

Given

To understand
the eternity of all
that is given
when we realize
the beauty of it all
is provided
when we
share the all
given
by the
creator of it all
lovely
thru our
understanding
provided
day today
Beautifully-we've
Got the picture.

Birthdays

Birthdays
for the young
surprise bells of many
yet...
To be rung.
Birthdays
for the old
surprise bells-of few
yet
to be rung
most
already...
Ring, rang, rung.
Oh those Birthdays.

Of Life

Across the
stepping stones
of life
many walk beside us
that we cannot see
for they have left
but we know
and feel silently
that they, there be
thru a soft love
constantly...
Across the stepping stones
of life.

Rough

This I've seen
the very young
do some time
when things get
very rough
in the quiet
they put their
head down
and they cry
get back in the race
and they
just fly.
This
I've seen
the very young
do sometime.

Tricycle

Legs too short
to touch the
tricycle pedals
my oh my-what
can you do.
Why you sit
on the tricycle
walk with the tricycle
move with the tricycle
that's what I seen
one child do.
She got there too
with her legs to
short to touch
the pedals.

Rebirth

If you love-really love
it never really disappears
its always around its near
its like snow that melts
it never really leaves
its always around
it just melts-goes in to
the ground-makes helps
plants grow-things
that live in the ground
thrive move around
helps grass green things
to grow life move too
if you love some one
really love-tho
even tho, they leave
they're still around
in mem-or-ry,
they move thru life
thru loved ones
too loves strong
as civilizations-snow
that disappears in to the
earth loves always around
like miracles
love thrives
for...it has-rebirth.

Discerning

The lonesome cry
heard mountain high
but only by the ear
or the discerning eye
that understands
the call, when made-
of the lonesome cry.

Honestly

Temper, temper
if it flies
it can hurt
as bees that fly
temper, temper
kept within
can burn as fire
from within
temper, temper
must be kept
as oceans keep tides
controlled
religiously
honestly.

Here

Tonight,
I felt you come
to visit
I felt your presence
here
the dogs next door
perhaps they seen you
they barked and
whined real lonesome
like
and when I felt you left
they stopped then too.
Come visit any time
you want
I love your presence
here.
And tonight when
you came to visit
I felt your presence
here.

White Owl

A great white owl
in faint moonlight
one night
flew slow
as you please
thru the trees-stopped,
and peeked
at me below
with ease.
at my campsite
A great white owl
in faint moonlight

Taxes

Paid my taxes
the others day
every body
sooner or later
pays them some way
their way.
have to pay taxes
in some way
just to live here
every day.
Paid my taxes
the other day.

Do

We do
what we can do
as long
as we can do
what we are to do
that's all that we
can do
and
thank you.

Move On

You feel a stare
you turn around
some one is there
looking at you.
You are alone
you feel strong
very strong
some one is there
with you
you turn around
check everywhere
no one, but you.
You feel
you stare
move on-you do
you have to...yet,
No– one is there.

Work Long

Be strong
to work
be happy
never stop
work long
and longer
too
be strong
to work is good
there's always
much
to do.

Special

The very special way
you grow a year
just in a day.
Is when you
have a birthday
and when it
goes away
and...
Happy birthday
on
that very special
day.

Something

Sometime
to want to do
something
can't
think of
what to do
time keeps-passing by
like little
flying flies
as the mind
keeps thinking
too.
Is kind of like
the dawn-is peeking
right as night
is thru.
To want to do
something
can't
see thru
or...
Think of
just...
What to do.

Tag

Never play tag
with the waves
of the ocean
when they
crash, crash, crash
on the shore
you never can win
from the waves
of the ocean
there's always
more waves more
that will come-carry you
far far away, real far away
far very far
from the shore
never-ever
play tag
with the waves of the ocean
they never play
with the shore.

A Time

There comes a time
when one from two
is one
and one must do the same
as two before has done.
When this time has come
it brings lonesome too
to help you thru
but lonesome in its way
keeps you lonesome
night and day
lonesome and busy are not friends
in any kind of way.
when the time for one from two
it comes for you
keep busy in the place
with you
lonesome will stay far
from you.

Thank You

Very silent-this poem, word by word
came to me-from one
I know
not from or anyone
can anymore-ever see
for they now rest in eternity.
The poem you read
the song you sung
was heard
transferred
and completely
understood
appreciated too
the whole way thru
much more
than you really
understood
thank you
thank you
you don't know
but I was there
the poem you read
the song you sung
I seen it
too.

A Park

Go park
in a park sometime
and just park
a park is a nice place
to park
go park
in a park.

Maybe

One never knows
they never do
how long friend's come here to stay
you never do
some stay for many years
they really do
some stay a short time
that they do.
Some leave early
by
they them selves
their way
just why-we most times
never know
why to this them selves they do
one
may never really know
and perhaps one's not supposed
to know
the creator does tho
how long one's come
here to stay
and life it self
maybe
flows better
also,
with love...in its way
tho sometimes most times
all times-when
one leaves
memories come,memories stay
life's way...
too memories-do.

Night Comes

When the sun has-had its stay
and sets to rest-from
work of day.
Then night comes
with artificial light
the moon and stars
of night
come out-if one is
all alone
lone some
then too
to help you in a lonesome way
and the night slips thru
as lonesome soothes you
lonesome way
you may even holler
if you do that is good
its good for you
do something anything good
that you can do
keep busy
busy pushes lonesome
end over end
and away
when the sun has gone its way
and night time comes
to stay.
And dark brings quiet
quiet has a tone
if one is alone one adjusts
with the night
thru its tone.

A Picture

Paint a picture
draw a picture
make a picture
any way you
make a picture
the picture is.
You-your thoughts.
it tells of you
the picture is you.

Changes

Autism
autism
autism
creeps in silent slow
in a way.
And changes
some folks
day-to- day
and in a completely
different...
Autism
way.
Much like fog foggy days.

Raining

Sleeping when its raining
is a pleasant thing
to do
you get a soothing
personal contentment
from the rain soft
coming down
and a silent something
that while you rest
a something is being
sent with love
meant especially
just for you.
And if when you
awaken
a rain bow's shining
too.
wow...
Lucky you.
rain
while sleeping
and
a rain bow
too.

The Sky

Rows of clouds
in the sky-I see
rows and rows
of clouds
way way up high
in the sky
all white and moving
way way up high
rows and rows
of clouds
and the sky is blue
where the clouds
are too
blue sky
clouds of white
in the sky
of
blue.
Rows and rows
of color
in the sky.

Night Time

The dark, the dark
where the sun don't shine
and the meadow lark sleeps
because its night time
and the street lights shine
and there's light in the park
the moon and the stars
just light up the sky.
People still walk
some ride by
everything else is the same
as in day
and when daytime comes
you can see its that way
some people quiver
and they shiver some
because of the dark
but dark is just dark
because theres no light
dark does no harm
others do harm
dark has no way
when day light comes
dark goes away
the dark, the dark
where the sun don't shine
and theres light in the park.
In the dark-the dark.

Hot

The weather
is
quite hot today
the children
only want to play
today.

Kinda

That song
just kinda
in a way
ringed a bell
to back then
in a way
and kinda waked
a something-in my mind
a kinda way
that song in a way
touched something
brought back
a long ago
from quite sometime ago
maybe 60-maybe 70 years
or more
that song-that song
just kinda-in a way
ringed a bell
from a long way back
and-from
way, before.

Cool

Waters cool
in the
water pool
water kinda
feels
so good
when its hot
very hot
in
the cool
water pool.

Blue

A little white airplane
just flew by
way up high
in the clear
blue sky
the sky was just
so blue, blue, blue
when the airplane
flew.
I don't know
where the airplane
went
in the sky
the sky
of
blue, of blue.

Around

All the bad
things
you just said.
When I left
I tilted my head
spilled then out
on the ground
no need to
carry
all those bad
things
you just said
around.

Along

when the dawn
has come
and the sunshine to
and the moon
don't shine
because the sun is too
and the stars-don't shine
because the sun
is bright
and there is no night
night is gone.
another day has come
just let it happen
try to enjoy it
things like this
happen
after dawn
just float a long
when the dawn
has come.

Back

I went back
just to see
how far
far back
could be,
and a song
took me.
Just for free.
That was neat
just neat
as neat could be

See

To see-to see
is simply
beautiful-and
to understand
all that you see
not many
this...
can really do
so
to see-to see
is wondrous
too
but be careful
what you stop
to see
for it can
peek and tell
on
you.

They Know

Computing
computers
they know about you
folks have
entered all
the information
they know
about you.
You better be careful
those
computing
computers
they, know about you.

Watched

Grieving, grieving
goodly-goodly
dangerous too
brings temper with it
when it comes
thru
it must be...tho
when its time
arrives
to keep all within
its reach alive
but
grieving, grieving
goodly goodly
dangerous too
must be-watched-controlled
when its time
comes thru.

Older

The young they wonder
how older can be
they then think
that never could happen
to me.
But then-as grass
is green in the spring
and as autumn draws nigh
the grass is no longer
full green
soon spring season
no longer one sees
and then the young wonder
no longer.
For the secret is there.
all can see-just how
older can be.

Thinking

Your sub-consciousness
mind is thinking
it is thinking
all the time
it can make things
happen
that seem true
to you
things you think
things you do
that you might even do
too.
It can do it-does
all the time.
your sub-consciousness
mind is thinking
it is thinking
all the time.

Meadows

Follow paths thru the forest
to meadows, quaint houses
where flowers bloom
and birds thru open skies,with
sunshine, fly
there full moon of round.
With light of silver
shines in deep
of dark night sky
follow the trees
cross mountains, valleys
on a path
thru the forest
to these meadows
of sunshine
meadows of flowers where birds fly
and house's are close by quaint houses
thats where the lovely lies.

Strange

Strange things
strange things
they happen everyday
strange things
strange things
they make an
in-ter-est-ing,day
strange things
strange things
could happen to you or me
most any of the
strange things
strange things-strange things
that we see
strange things
strange things
they happen every day
strange things
strange things
strange things
many
strange things
they make an
in-ter-est-ing
day.

A Time

There comes a time
in time
when one from two
is one
and now I must do the same
almost,
as two before has done
and that is...now
when one from two is one
there comes a time in time
the time is now
when this time
is done
I must accept...
This time-has come.

Red Dress

Dresses,dresses
seems there's-many a kind
about whatever
the heart may desire
and still be kind.
but I liked
the red dress
that lady had on
because it brought out
a something
the eyes could dwell on
that red dress
the lady had on.
There's dress of feathers
there's dress for a bird
the way they wear them
when they prance and dance
a dance of love
and prance and dance
and dance
but I liked the red dress
that lady had on
because it brought out
a something
the eye could dwell on
the red dress
that lady had on.

Gone

Sunshine's gone
for today
only, so much
sunshine
for each day
sunshine's today
no more, if you want
more sunshine
wait for tomorrow
borrow.
Some sunshine
and...
think of
today.

Boot-Toot

Bootsile tootsie
bootsie tootsie
bootsie tootsie
too
tootsie bootsie
tootsie bootsie
tootsie bootsie
woo
bootsie tootsie
bootsie tootsie
bootsie tootsie
who
are you?
tootsie bootsie
tootsie bootsie
bootsie tootsie
tootsie bootsie
tootsie tootsie
toot, toot-boot-boot
I am me.

Finished

Vacations finished
gotta teach the body
work time again
no more
sleepin in
no more loafin
all day
cause that's
simply not the way
not now...
its work time
vacations finished
gotta teach the body
hey body
hey hey-say-say
body...
its
work time ,again.

Bimbley Bimbley

Timbley, bimbley,boo
I think that
I see you
bimbley, bimbley, bimbley
bimbley, bimbley
boo
hootley, hootley who
hootle'y hootley who
hootley, hootley who
is that you
yes, this me
this is me
that you see-that you see
hootley, bimbley
bimbley, hootley
hootley, bimbley
this
be me...ooo-eee, whee
this be me.

Its Way

Silence is quiet
but speaks its way
some
understand
some
answer
some do
as
they pass thru
and...
hear silence
total silence
speak
its way.

Celestial

Thru a
restaurant
window
I see
a sky of blue
a flag
of
red-of
white
and blue
waving, softly
waving, waving
thru the
window
I can also
feel
a celestial
love from
the quiet
sky of
blue.
That feels
lovely
lovely, lovely
and so...so very
very, real.

New Day

When most things
finish
they are forever
gone.
Except
for a day.
because-tomorrow
there's always
tomorrow,
and
tomorrow
a new day
comes
along.

The Days

Endings make new beginnings
of most things
if we observe
as we travel along
like notes of a song
they have rythmn
in movement
of life
thru ups and downs
in goodness and strife
all need be done
is open life's windows
when doors close
and theres the sun
each day
with new of days
being offered.
Endings make new beginings
of most things.
We must make.
new the ways-with...the days.

Bloom

Not trained
to bloom
in the spring
but bloom anytime some plants
that nature
may bring
are noticed too
and when they do
they...
Bring happiness
at the time
to whomever their
beauty
comes to.

You and Me

Water, water
wet is water
wet as it can be
water water
Do you like water?
that wets
you and me.
Water water
I like water
all the water
I can see
water water
for everything
like ships, and boats
at docks that float
and in the deep
deep water be.
For everyone
to see.
Water water
wet is water
wet as it
can be
and...water
its good
for
you and me.
Water,water
water.
Do you like
water?

Could Be

For you to be
a stranger to you...
Could-my friend
could be
if you will it to be
try hard to be
could be-my friend
could be.
Your world-tho
would be small
very so very small
almost
no world at ail
my friend
almost
no world at all
if you will it to be
try hard to be
could be-my friend
could be.
Try hard
to never feel or be
a stranger-to you
to your self always be
true to you
that is a very beautiful
things to do
and-could be, my friend
it could be
the very beautiful
it could be.

This Land

Never forget
to
celebrate
on independence
day
vote your choice
on
election day
that
you have
equal
opportunity
in this land
under law
to do
and accomplish
anything
honest-good
and true.
Also…
never forget
in this land
you must
work
very, very hard
long hours
in most everything
to accomplish
this
and be happy
too.
But…
you can do this
many...
Have done this
here,
never-forget.

The Ride

Ride the waves
ride the waves
ride the waves
till the waves
hit the shore.
The waves go back
and the ride is then no more
deal with whatever
you brought, with you
on the waves
on the ride
to the shore.

They

When birds mingle together
talk quiet
their way
we never know
the least
what they say.

Each Day

The tides come and go
each day
changing the shore lines
ever ever slight
day by day.
And the moon-moves the same
its effects quite same
tho
creation knows why.
All causing
each day to be same
and
ever slight-indifference
too.
As the tides, the moon
each day-with nights
move
quietly
creations way...
Thru.

Maybe

By the ocean today
I watched
as the pelicans flew
so graceful-they fly
and quietly
too.
I think, maybe
the sky watched
and maybe...
It did
too.
by the ocean today
its way.

Their Wings

The birds
flap their wings
from low
to high.
And then they
soar and soar
in the open sky.

Observed

The things we do
maybe observed
as different
but yet much
the same
in many ways
to do
so many many
ways and play
paint and start
the finish to
of the many
things we do
in love
with love
the things we do.
That observed
make's us
what we are
from
what we
do-in,
the things-
the many things
we do.

Explaining

Seems like everything
done each day-now
is leading to something
each day
don't know what it
must be
as long as it is good
honest and true
will go along-and
follow thru
seems like each day
comes with love
in its way
explaining-if one listens
that's the right thing
to do it
this way.

Songs

Listening to songs
of long ago
I was transported back
and lovely too
to long ago
and back again
to where
I started from
Quietly too...
just
listening to songs
songs-songs
has a way
of doing that
to many people
songs
songs-do.

Sometime

Some time the entire day
will go by
and a word-not
a single word is spoken
not a word to anyone
except to me by me
as the world not bothered
flows by.
and…I think of the world
as the world perhaps,
ponders me
as sometime
the entire day
goes by.
not a word, why?

Dreams

Thru our dreams
sometime we see
the beautiful
the sad
are naught
but empty
and forget fullness
of thought.
And thru our dreams
sometime we see
a nothing
to remember
or fullness
of love
to see
our dreams
given to each
so faith fully.
thru our dreams
so much
sometime
we see.
just seen-thru our dreams

The Past

Friends of the past
that you once know
of years gone by
are some what
as birds thats flown by
and difficult
when remembered
just how-and in
the year of now
how to locate
and see-how they
may be
perhaps they too
may remember may ponder
now in the December
of years
as they flow-with slow by
just where-just how
that friends of past
may be-and if
sometime, it maybe
possible to meet
and each other
visit...and see.
For friends these thoughts pass.
maybe-
from friends, friends of the past

Moving

The clouds-are moving
to one side
of the sky
so blue-can color
the rest of
the sky.

Summer

The month of June
is finished
the middle
of July is now here.
And July has a way
of rushing thru to
august.
Then august slips
fast thru
to September
the home of
autumn
with no room
for summer
from the month
of June "(not-anywhere)"
so summer
say's
bye
good bye
I'm leaving
good bye.

Wagon

Push the wagon
pull the wagon
roll the wagon
here
we want the
wagon back-now.
So roll the wagon
here
Do you hear?
Roll the wagon
here.
Thank you.

Because

When ever you want to
just talk to the man
in the mirror
he'll talk right back to you
be good
to the man in the mirror
he'll be good-right back to you
get angry
with the man in the mirror
he'll get angry right back to you
be nice
to the man in the mirror
he'll reason as you reason
with you.
Treat the man in the mirror
as your neighbor
he'll be a good neighbor
with you.
When ever you want to
just talk to the man in the mirror
he'll look right at you
always be honest
and talk right back to you.
Because…
you are the man
in the mirror
so...always...
be honest-with you.

Wow

When all seemed worse
no matter what
things get
worse and worse
dark was dark
and darker still
it seemed there was
no light
worse, worse, worse
all got worse
thunder, lightning
too
then
bam...
When
things got-halfway
no matter what
wow...
See you later.

Focus

Focus on the bad
is easy
to be had
focus on the good
is sometime
mis understood
the good-is better
tho
bad is easy
to be had
don't focus on the bad.

The Forever Train

Careful of the train
you get on
don't get on the
forever train
it never ever stops
for any thing
the track never breaks
it don't need fuel
no engineers or folks
are there
no stations on its run
it just goes on and on
and on
it never ever gets there
you never get old
you never get young
you just get on
and there you are there
careful of the train
you get on
don't get on the
forever train
you never will get there.

Three

The little girl
with long blonde curls
and she was only three
she ran-she ran
she run
she never knew
what tired was
she'd stop a few
seconds
and then she'd go
tired she did not know
the little girl
that was only three
smiling running
happy
just...
Happy as she could be.

A Picture

One day
I took pictures
with my camera
of friends
I know
in other places
many years ago
only the pictures now-I have
they connect
with the friends
in a way
tho the friends
I know not
not or where
are they.
The friends in the picture
I took
with my camera
many years ago
one day.

Afraid

The rain-the rain
some people are afraid
of the rain
the rain sometime
has lightning and thunder
wind with it to
the rain is just water
that don't matter
some people are still
afraid of rain
too
how about you?
are you afraid of
the rain-the rain
are you afraid of the
rain?.

Windy

Bubbles on a
windy day
bubbles on
windy day
bubbles, bubbles
bubbles, bubbles
bubbles on a
windy day
blow high
and fly away.
Thats what bubble do
when you make
bubbles, bubbles
bubbles, bubbles
bubbles on a
windy day.

Seen

Today I seen
an airplane fly
off in a sky of blue
and away
the airplane never
did come back
I hope there
are lights
in the sky of blue
where the airplane
went today
it really does
get dark
way up in the sky
when the sunlight "(goes away)"

Time to Time

In my dreams-I see
sometime
those who're left
from time to time
dreams seem real
when they come too
and then they vanish
after they've came thru
leaving memory
of
times past-of now
and some of those to come
some how
dreams are beautiful
in their way
explaining with mystery
their magical
touch.
in my dreams sometime
I see
those who're left and those whov'ed lived
from time-to time.

Never Ever

Go
down to the ocean
see
far far away
to
where the waters-seem to be
touching the sky
and then
travel
over waters
to the ends-of the earth
and ne'er ever
touch
the sky.
and that
in its way,
will
have to
satisfy.

Multiply

Dig a hole-with help
for nearly
60 years-and stop
then take the help away
and fill the hole
little by little
to smooth be
nice but-slow
some each day
your way.
This must be done
and should be done
by each one
in different ways
differently-smooth by
digging holes and filling holes
as years flow by-as days go by
as love it self
does multiply.
creating the valleys
of life
as life multiplies
flowing by,

Things We See

The clouds
the few
the sunshine too
and stars
and moon-so high
they help, to make
up all
the many
beautiful
mysterious
things we see
in the heaven
oh,
so high.

The Bridge

Beneath the bridge
the water flows
bringing clean water
and dirt that flows by
on the bridge all passes
the clean, the dirt
for the mind the eye
to love clean water
is easy
to love dirty water
takes time
takes friends
tests love
the choice is either
as to the glimpse
clean clear water and dirt
flow by daily
beneath the bridge
for the glimpse of the eye
In our worlds bridges
and our minds
flowing-flowing
always
flowing.
Daily flowing by.

Probably

Since I'm an over
80 years old
and you are not
I can't do most
of what you do
and you probably
don't want
to do
what I do
so...
Lets each be fair
and let each
pass quietly
thru
as we are.

Gotta Watch

The boys, the boys
the boys said
the dinosaurs ate
all the rabbits
and all the squirrels too
they said the dinosaurs
do this
when the dinosaurs
come thru.
And the boys said
the dinosaurs don't ride
skate boards, bicycles
but, they take great big steps
when they walk
that takes then very far
and don't forget...the boys said
that they-also-eat
squirrels and rabbits
so-you
really gotta-watch
the dinosaurs…
When they
come thru.

Quite Well

A turtle-a turtle
stays in his shell
and only comes out
when things only go quite well
sometimes
that might be,
a good way to see
the world
have it move
a long
more smooth-ill-ly
like
a turtle, a turtle
who
stays in his shell.

84

Hill

There's a little hill
in the road
in my mind-I see
bout 1/4 mile away
and a sharp curve
to the right-there
I am told the highway
is tough bumpy
rest of the way
to straight a head
again to a main highway
hard to tell tho
as high way minds go.
And little hills-in the
mind-makes the
thinkin flow
bumpy sometime...
lifes that way,
tho.
lots of
hills and curves
and bumps

Cat

The cat
is company
and in her way
wakes little
sleeps most
of the day
away.

Something

There is something
that was
in this house-that's
not here anymore
and it seems
I have to leave
at times
to go and go-to
just explore
and look, and look
but not find-or want to find
I guess
because...
in my mind
the something that
was in this house
before
I feel that at this
time of history
with me
could never ever find again,
and...
that's the way
it goes
old buddy roe
that's the way...
it goes.
now-anyway.
Tho history is strange-
strange indeed.
and see, and...pass
things-thru.

So

Have wasted the
night away
now sunshine is here
to stay all day
sleep you have to do
shared with sunshine too
and sleep is something
all must do
to keep a body happy
also, functioning too
be more careful
with night
don't just waste it away
night time must be used
same as
time of the day
or it seems
more quickly to fade
fast away
so-you
have wasted then night away
sunshine is here today to stay.
All day now...
Just.deal with it.
you have wasted
this night away.

Quiet

Afternoon
a quiet one too
a blue sky
a little clouds
way off
in the corner-the far corner
of the world staying
just to kind of
fill up the sky.
Just finished eating
at a little eatery
too.
Rest of the afternoon
seems passing beautiful
just slipping
quiet thru
with blue sky
a little clouds
with sunshine
a little lazy
my way
flowing, soft
country stream like
thru.
a quiet,quiet
afternoon

Pleasantly

To be visited in dreams
by someone whom
has left
that you know
is quite lovely
and with life
does
very pleasantly
flow.

For You

Spiritual help
from the creator
is there for you
anytime-any day
to see and help
you thru.
All you need do
is ask as you would
of a very good
friend
and tell of your need
also
to the creator be true
spiritual help
from the creator
is there for you
anytime-any day
to see, and help
you thru.

Congregate

Together-together
like families do
or
like families should do
is a most
beautiful way
to communicate
when families
congregate
together-together
like families do
is a most
beautiful way
to remember

Kick Back

I've got nothin to do
to fill up my day
except sit around
write
and pass time
away.
The sun's shinin
tho
mornings
passed thru
so guess-i'll just
eat a small snack
kick back
write
doze, a little too
and pass
a lovely
afternoon
twilight, evening
thru.
I've got nothin else
to do.

It Talks

Your house
it talks to you
its special way
as years go by
it knows you too
it has its way
you'll listen too
when its quiet-quiet
when things happen
good or bad
it'll talk-your house
in
squeaks, squawks, scunch, scratch
sounds to you
you'll understand
when...
your house
it talks to you.

Seventeen

If
when one were
seventeen
one could change
ones world
for-say
sixty years
ahead
as they
desired-it be
how beautiful
it would be.
But all
must wait
for that
if given
to...be.

My My

When the grand daughters
came
the days passed by
my, my-how they
seemed to fly
with only one here
the days seem spaced far
at times
like mile stones are
but when
grand children come
like when
grand daughters came
the days pass by
my, my-how they
seemed to fly.

Wee Little

I have
a wee little
flashlight
with only
one battery too
it does a lovely job
of doing
what it was made
to do
of piercing dark
with very bright
light
to shine
thru,dark.
I have
a wee little flashlight
with only
one battery
I like very much
and that
I do.

A Memory

With everything there is
a something-that
in its way
creates a memory
that comes to stay.
And when called upon
its special way
will remind us
softly-quietly
I'm still here, | came to stay
here with your memories
if you need me call me
anytime
and soft, quiet
as flowers in a meadow
clouds on high
the memory fades
like a rainbow after rain
little trace it came
with everything-that
in its way
creates a memory.
And…
Most are lovely.

To See

The sky is beautiful
to see
its there for free
for all to view
Sometimes…
look at it too.
the sky is beautiful
to see
if you do.

The Bank

The bank of time
you are given
every day
to be used-in a way
to
help the mind
and body stay
healthy
in relation to
the world around
each day.
To help your neighbor
others too
the same as
you-your self you
as you
pass thru.
In what way
do you use
the bank of time
you are given
every day ?

Near

When a loved one
leaves forever
their love is forever
near
as the sunshine
that surround us
as the stars so far
but near
and the love is felt
to each so
differently
so soft as drifting
clouds
in heaven high
yes...
When a loved one
leaves forever...
their love is forever,
near.

In Salinas

That's what I like
about California
at least the part
where I live in Salinas
there's always the close
distant surround of mountains
and when in evenings
or maybe
especially in evening
tho clouds maybe low
and sky is blue
the mountain tops
framed against sky of blue
with sunshine too
gives silent beauty
quite special at close of day
as another day
passes thru
I like that about California
its always there
its free too, for all
to view.

Weather

Today is cool
yesterday
was warm
the day before
the weather
was hot
some folks
might say
what the weather
will be
but the weather
might change
then again
it might not
like
today is cool
yesterday warm
the day before
the weather
was hot.

A Slippin

He's a slippin
he's a slippin
he's not doin
what we feel
he's supposed
to do
let's see-if we
can help
him thru.
We can see-and
We feel
he's a slippin
he's a slippin
he's not doin
what we feel
he's supposed
to do.
He's a slippin

A Hawk

I seen a hawk
a big-big bird
go soaring by
hardly moving its wings
but flying high
tho
not too high
in the sky.
Looking close, for food
from in the sky
I just seen
This hawk...
a big big bird
go soaring by-real quiet too,
hardly moving its wings
looking close for food
from
in the sky, a sky, of blue.
I seen a hawk
a big big bird
soaring by.

Do

Do the best
you can do
in
what ever you do
because...
That's all you
can do
in all
you do
is
the best
you
can do
never-ever
forget...
to-do
the
very-very
"best you can do."

That Night

While camping
one night
I did see
in the moon light
thru the trees
high over me.
Peeking down at me
with huge wings outspread.
A great white owl
I often-wonder
what that owl
did see.
Perhaps-twas
just me
while camping
that night
in the moonlight.

Today

Its Wednesday
the middle
of the week
the week's
all go this way
if...
the middle
of the week
was on
another day
it would
probably be
this way
too-so...
lets keep
the middle
on
Wednesday
have to have
a middle
like Wednesday
is today
to get the week
all the way
thru.

A Chain

A link-a link
the weakest link
yes...
The strongest chain
will break, oh break- if,
the weakest link, breaks ... it destroys,
the strongest chain.

Tea

Get a package
of
moo-gee-cha-tea
moo-gee-cha-tea
moo-gee-cha-tea
drop it
in
a pitcher
of water
a pitcher
of water
let it sit-for
about an
hour
makes
moo-gee-cha-tea
moo-gee-cha-tea
moo-gee-cha-tea
then-drink
moo-gee-cha-tea
moo-gee-cha-tea
moo-gee-cha-tea
for...
moo-gee-cha-tea
is
very-good-tea
very-good-tea
very-good=tea
and
moo-gee-cha-tea
moo-gee-cha-tea
moo-gee-cha-tea

continued

is
good-for-thee
good-for-thee
good-for-thee
drink-drink-drink
drink-drink-drink
lots-of
cups-of
good-fresh
moo-gee-cha-tea
moo-gee-cha-tea
moo-gee-cha-tea
its
good-good good
good-for-thee
drink-drink
moo-gee-cha-tea
moo-gee-cha-tea
moo-gee-cha-tea.

Talking

Sometime
on the telephone
we can-do some
talking talking
talking
over the old
and new
times
again.
remembering-remembering
thru,
the fog-of years
sometime.

Beautiful

To remember the morning
in a beautiful way
the moon
the twilight
evening
night too.
Is the way
that
another day
has came thru
to you
to be remembered
in a
beautiful-way.

Flying By

A pelican-a pelican
I see
a pelican-flying by
between the earth
and,
the sky.

All Day

Its been cloudy
All day
Now the sun´s
Coming out
I see long shadows
Too.
Twilights coming soon
It needs some
Sunshine too
That's what
Days usually
Have
And its nice
Because...
Its been cloudy
All day
And now, evenings here
The suns – coming out too.

Scooters

People with scooters
Use one foot
To stand –
On two feet
They roll,
Then with one
Foot
They hop
With two feet
They roll
Again
Having fun
Till they stop
People with scooters
Doing the
Hoppity, hoppity
Roll along - fun,
Scooter art.

Brings

Along, along
when something good
comes along
it brings
as notes
of
a beautiful
song.
to many
and few-something, of an opportunity
They may have.
waited long for
when something good
along.

View the Ocean

The ocean-the ocean
I never tire
of viewing the ocean
with its constant
speech
its roar
seems it always
speaks of much
there's always much
there
to listen-view
see explore
the ocean-the ocean
seems many too.
just...
View the ocean.

Clouds Move

On a hazy cloudy day
viewing from the shore
where the sky
meets the sea
appears-to move
close to far away
as the clouds
move
their way
on a-hazy cloudy day.

Waiting

All the world
is waiting
to see you do
that
what you,
can do.
so start
if it is good
and do
that
what you
can do
all the word
is waiting.

Discuss

The pelicans
and many birds
fly together
when they fly by.
Maybe they
discuss together
what they see
as they fly
when they fly by.

For You

A nice day
for a birthday
a birthday
for you.
Happy birthday
happy birthday
to you
birthdays are nice
birthdays are nice.

Ours-Hours

Hours hours
they
are
ours.
Each
60
minutes
one
goes
by.
They seem
to fly
and...
Hours are ours
to use
for good
if we try.

A Campfire

While a campfire
burns
with light
in dark of night
unseen...
A great white owl
with wings
out spread
hovers motion less
at tree top
level
peering
with great interest
at those below
while,
the camp fire burns
with light
in dark of night.
then...
the wise old owl
quietly-flies way
from the campfires light
in the dark of night.
having seen how
people live in the night.

A Bird

If a bird-in a tree
looked down
at me and said
how do you do
How are you
today?
I'd look back
and say
I'm fine-to the bird
I'm fine today
and how are you-feeling today?
that's what i'd say
to the bird-in the tree
that looked down
at me.
What would you say?

Birds

If you could go
sit in a tree
is that where
you would like to be?
No birds-they sit
in trees, not me -not me
but if you sit
in a tree
then you from high
could see
where you all day
now see.
No thanks
I'll stay right have
now please
tweet-twitter
that
to the birds, and you...
go sit-in a tree.

Bumpity

At the top
of the slide
are two bumps
waiting for you
half way down
theres one
and at the bottom
of the slide
there's
another two.
On a ride
from top
to bottom
of the slide
there's
another two
on a ride
from top
to bottom
of the slide
you go...
Bumpity,bumpity
bumpity,bumpity
bump
on a real nice
bumpity
fun ride
from top
to the bottom
of the slide.

The Sunflowers

And all
the children
came to see
the sunflowers
with leaves
of green
any yellow
growing tall
over the
fence tops
where all
could see
the pretty
sunflowers
every one just
loved the
flowers-and,
all the children
came
to see...
The sunflowers.

In Sight

Fighting-fighting-fighting
they're fighting
every body in sight.
why are they
fighting, fighting, fighting?
they don't know
no body knows
but-they're
just...
Fighting, fighting, fighting
fighting every body...
every body in sight.

Wonderfully

I see beauty in
the blue of sky,
and drifting cloud
today.
And you say-you see beauty
in the flowers-trees
green of grass
today-now
if I see, feel, and think
only half of what
you see, feel and think
and you can do the same
for me
why together we can see
and feel
the beauty in most things
quite, wonderfully.

A Conversation

They say it cannot be
for those who're
gone away-to
forever stay
to converse with us
in their way
when needs be
but I think that
maybe this
is so
and perhaps
an understanding, conversation
in this way
can be
also...
countless others
think like
me
how bout you?

Open Air

Out where
there's open air
no walls anywhere
there's trees too
to look down on you
and wave branches
that the moon
at night-peeks thru
to view down on you
where a campfire at night
can, crackle, pop
and hiss
while it roast's corn
chicken meat
a steak
hot dog-and bun
and you can-in fun
relax for some days,
and nights
of camping
out where
there's just open air
no walls any where
and
there's trees too
while you kick back-and let
the world-slip by
tis a great place
to see-to be.
out where there's
open air and no walls
anywhere.

But the Way

Creation dresses
the mountains valleys
flowers, meadows
the sky so fair
the lady
in the red dress
could never...ever
compare.

Some Low

Hatred and evil
they are close
and the same almost
except by name
we have them around.
They have been
here for years
centuries back
no good in either
both words lack good
hatred hath evil
evil hath hatred
they both have this
in each
and both exist
very much
even now
with their hatred, evil
touch…
for some reason
and quite active
they live on,on and on-
Some how...
why-why.

Light

The north star
shines bright
with its guiding light
to follow
as it guides thru
the brambles and clutter
of earth below
to desire's of
the hearts delight
follow
the north star
with its guiding
heavenly
light.

A Bee

A bee flew in
my camping van
this morning
I let it out
it flew away.
Its evening now
the bee-or
its relation
looked in the
window
a few minutes
ago
maybe it wanted in
for the evening
I glanced back
perhaps
the bee
got the message
no bees welcome here
anytime
especially wearing
a yellow jacket
like the bee
was wearing
that flew in
my camping van
this morning.

A Roar

The ocean
speaks to the shore
thru its waves
with a roar.

An Afternoon

In the afternoon, that summer afternoon
sunshine came
and some blue
came thru in
the sky...brought joy
then clouds, of white
drifted by
covering the sunshine
and blue, of sky
on that summer day
cool came too
twilight-evening came
the afternoon went
it went...taking the joy
and left
from the sky
night arrived
soon
with dark
leaving only memories
of
an afternoon
of
blue sky
that-briefly-came
our way
that summer
day.

Water

To just sit – and watch the ocean
Watch the ocean – water,
Have its way
Send its waves – softly splash
Its shorelines
In a graceful – patterned way
With a sky – just a show of gray
Sunshine not yet – brightly,
Shining thru.
To just sit and watch the ocean
With others there
Playing, watching too.
I think...
Is a most relaxing
And satisfying
Thing to do
While the seagulls, pelicans
Just gracefully
Fly by.
I think – maybe – in their way
They watch the ocean
At its play, have its way, too.

A Tent

Today
I watched
A man
Putting up – his tent
He carefully
Tightened the ropes
And poles
As he went
Then
When he finished
The tent
Looked strong
And...
It appeared
He might
Be humming
A happy tent song
Today
As I watched
A man –
Put up his tent.

Every Day

Flying-low
over the ocean
the pelicans
play
they play
that-way
every day.

One

With
youth oh youth
one
fly-eth
by
and-with
age
one
walk-eth
by.

Dark

The,
Dark is strange
No shadows there
The,
Dark is strange
It... only,
Reigns –
There.

Free

Long shadows
Of the evening
Sunsets
On its way
Comes every
Single day
And its free
For you –
And
Me.

The Moon

Say…
there's the moon
in the sky tonight
with its light
I looked out the patio door
tonight
thru the door glass
I seen the moon
alone in the sky
in the dark tonight
the only real big
light in the sky
at its home, by night
its home
for hundred's-thousands
of years.
if it could say worlds
or play music-of
what its seen, its way
for us to hear or be near
it would be most lovely
I'm sure coming
from the wise
ageless moon...
Lighting up the night
tonight.

Their Seeds

Dandelions when they dry
Fly like little
Feathers in the sky
Carrying their seeds
With them
As they fly in the sky
And when they
Touch the ground
They leave their seeds
Just all around
Soon new dandelions
Come
From the seeds
That's around all
And dandelions
When they dry
Fly like little
Feathers
With their seeds
In the sky.

Day

I waited and I waited
for an idea
to write about
till it came
smooth-ly,by
as time slow moved along
early morning
came too
and said hi
I'm bringing dawn thru
also-day is coming
along and today
why
it will be
just a lovely day
the idea then came
luscious splendid, and I wrote
about day
the most
beautiful, beautiful
simply
wonderful-day.

Fear

Lets see now
There's fear
Of –
Heights
Depth's
Flying
Diving
Death (that's probably the king of fears)
Oh yes...
Fear – of fear
Fear, fear
Its always near
Take a vacation
When you come back
Lets see now...
You maybe will find
Happiness to, in what you do
And faith with hope
Along the way, help you
Day to day.

That Way

To lose a race fairly
now thats ok
to not race-of fear
that one might lose
thats not ok
to do ones best
must be the rule
to live by
day to day
to lose or win
each race is won
or lost
fairly...
that way.

To Flow

When the life's blood
ceases to flow
its way
and the heart beat
stops its way
most animals shy
they keep distance...
and away.
a place in life
that one must be
changes then quite differently
for all to see-the day
when life's blood
ceases to flow
its way.

The Way

There's a
close ness
that comes
from some folks
and that
close ness does not fly
it stays right close near
when they leave
it does not disappear
like snow fall in the winter
stays till spring arrives
this close ness of them stays
and stays fills you helps
you in a way like sunshine
helps the strong then brings
out just the best in days
then some folks can
come you pass by in days
you see then speak and all
when leave its the same
like they just was a passing
breeze don't effect you
much at all
just almost like a
shadow on a wall.
Guess thats what makes
up life in a way-folks you meet, along the way
gives life substance
day by day.
And that helps step by
step to full paced walk
along the way.
Adds a closeness-to the day.

Almost Remember

It took a long time
for me to understand
that some time life
is not as kind
as we think
it should be.
I'll always remember
that day-the day
you left went away
April 15th I remember
that day
nearly two years soon
will have passed away
not long ago-I took
your pillow off the bed
put it away
and when I go to bed
I softly touch the spot
in the bed where you
always would lay
When I visit the cemetery
I always talk with you
We're together that way
its hard to understand the moves
of life sometime.
But our love is our love
the love we understand
and of creation
Our love is true it is...
that kind, that of love.

Shadow

A boy see's
his shadow
gives a little
kick too.
And his shadow
kicks then same...
like the boy
kicked, too. Boys and– shadows.

The Moon

Oh,
I can see
the glow of the moon
shining
over the mountain top
and while the moon is
climbing in the sky
stars are shining
just twinkling
all over the sky.
waiting for the moon
to climb up in the sky
the mountain is high
I hope the moon
can climb over the mountain
the stars and I
are waiting
waiting for the moon
because...
I seen-the glow of the moon.

Helps

Tho
I can't hear you
tho
I can't see you
I know you're gone
you left quite
some time ago
yet I know you're here
you're with me
I can feel your presence
tho
I feel your presence
tho
I can't see you
in your way in our way
you converse with me
I can feel your presence near
I love the feeling
too
it really helps
while traveling
thru.

David

Did you see David
We lost David
A bear, a bear, a bear
A teddy bear
With a blue jacket on
If you see David
We need David
He's been a long time gone
Everybody's looking
For
David David, David,
David with the blue
Jacket on
"Oh"
They found David, David, David
David the teddy bear
Cause...
David had a blue jacket
On
Cause... David had a blue jacket on.

Camping

I love to go
a camping
many families I see
while camping too.
Having special family
fun
creating memories lasting memories.
Thru love
and together, which lasts
for many days
many years.
A camping
a camping
together
making
together, just...
be fun.

From Fields

From farmers fields
and hard work
of few
is where most food
for the world
has grew
and hard work
in fields-is much
you see
it feeds the world
and you
and me.

Moving Picture

People walking
on the shore-with the ocean
right close by
their steps-I cannot hear
I'm sitting on a little hill
close by.
So to me
people walking-on the shore
with ocean birds
and ocean moving, roaring too
make a lovely moving
picture
as they move along
they do.

Only Three

Mommie – mommie
Please come
To me – you left me
Here at school
And I'm – only three
I'm just lonesome
As I can be
Its you – its you
That I want – to see
But many play things
And good things
To do here.- I see too
Nice people here
Maybe here soon –
I'll be ok
Come see me – don't forget me
Here at school
I love you
Mommie... mommie...

All Things

In all things
You do
Do your very best
To do the best
That you can do
And if what are you doing
Is good to do
A time will come
A place will come
A place will come
Where you
Will be rewarded
For all things that you may do
Creation, watches over you
And rewards
In special ways
For good and bad things
That you do
As are
All things
Done by you
As you pass thru.

To Roost

When all the chickens
Come home to roost
Where have
You been
To the chickens
Say we
We're been here, there
And everywhere
There's no room
Here – for all the chickens
Say we.
To many eggs to gather
Too.
Don't worry about eggs
The chickens say
We only beg
The chickens say,
Thats why we came home
To roost
We've now found...
Theres no other way
Go away – go away
Go away
Say we
When all the chicken's
Come home to roost.
some of you
are ok but not all
We've no place for you here to stay.

A leaf

When the month
Of October
Had come around
I found a leaf
From an old
Oak tree
Lying on the ground
As if it was saved
Maybe just
For me
I picked it up
The leaf – all golden brown
And saved the leaf
Pressed the leaf
Between leaves of
And old old book
To keep for years, and years
For free –
For others, and me
When the month
Of October
Had come around
The leaf
From the old
Oak tree
I found
Lying on the
Ground

Complain

Life is so strange
Has a wide wide of range
Leaves
Little room to complain
When we do
All we can do
With what life
Give us
We must do.

We View

When we view
The moon
Brightly shining
For all to see
By day
Its quite unusual
And not usual
And yet – its much
Of creation
Is always there
For us to view – to see
And yet – when
We view – the moon
By day the same moon
Is strange
To view by day
Perhaps –
When we view the moon
It must be done
By us – by night
And only the sun
By day.

Purple

Purple flowers
Purple flowers
Who oh who
Has purple flowers?
Do you mean
Those purple flowers
With the green leaves
Over on the fence?
Oh the fence – the fence
The fence – the fence
we have
The purple flowers
With the green leaves
That you seen.

A Hillside

If its a nice
Sunny day
When you're 4 years old
And not 2 or one
And you are on-
A grassy hillside
Not to high
And lay down on your side
In the grass
With your arms at your side
Then roll down the hill side
Slow – fast
Till you stop
In the grass
Its great fun – in the sun
And...
You maybe will get up
Go up the hill
And roll down
Once more
When you're 4 years old
Just playing
Having fun
In the grass – and...
The sun.

Your Heart

Follow your heart
What it tells
You
So silent – to do
You know
Only...
You know
Is telling you
Listen, listen
Its honest
With you –
In,
That you – should do
Follow on...your heart.

Pills

Theres a pill
For
Broken toes, and
Shin bones too
For creaky knees
Bad ankles too
For
Twisted hips and
Sore backs too
There are pills
For
Shoulders – necks
Headaches
And pills for
Almost anything
You can think of
And...
Pills help
If you think
They do.
When the pills – the pills
Are given,
To you.

To See

I'm writing a story
As it comes to me
Little by little
A story's way
A lot sometime
A little sometime
Not quite like a poem
A poem some places
Rhyme
A story does too
Sometime
And where imagery
Comes
The story does too
So I'm writing
A story, as it comes
To me –
Little by little
As stars come...
To see.

Those People

I wonder just what
those people
way over there
are doing?
Of course
its not my business
but...
I wonder-I wonder
Ever feel that way?
I'd still like to sneak
over there and see
Ever do that too?
I wonder what
those people
way over there,
are doing.

Sitting here

I'm sitting here
Among the flowers
Wild flowers – yellow flowers
That I see
They' re all around
With green of leaves
And yellow flowers
Decorating hill sides
For all to see
I'm sitting here
Among the flowers
Wild flowers - yellow flowers
Decorating hillsides
And I like, the flowers,
The flowers – I see.

Demands

Love demands
The all –
All the few
Can see.
Deeply in
Way down and in
The inner self
That few go see,
If love within stays,
Then love
Will shine
As sun shine does
For all to see
And loves
Demands
Will be wholly,
And true
For all and
You, and yes –
Me too.

Birthday

A sunshiny day
And Sunday too
A birthday cake
And friends around too
A lovely way
Also a very blessed day
For a birthday
Happy birthday

Helps you

Security of
Your home
Security where
You roam
Security where
You play
Security where you are
All day
And then nights too
Security – security
Helps you feel...
As a better, you.

Togetherness

A feeling of
Togetherness
Joins in a way
Those that are here
With
Those that are away
Thru
Writings, clothing
Pictures, feelings
Places absence too
Togetherness
In silence, together with thoughts
Connects mysteriously
In its way can bring thru
And
Joins spiritually in a way
Those that are here
With
Those that are away.

Flying

Today airplanes in the sky
Flying high
Are preparing for
An air show
Soon to come our way
Airplanes are prancing
And dancing
All over our skies
The sky in now almost
Crystal clear blue
But if the few clouds
Were made of rubber
Like tennis balls
The airplanes could bounce them
All over the sky
Like tennis balls
Because...
The airplanes – are flying
Fast and high
Prancing and dancing
Way up – in our sky
Today.

Suspended

Trees in the dark
Reaching for the sky
Yet...
Rooted, as one, small...
Such as I.
While the moon
Suspended – from the sky
Watches from a mountain top,
Nearby are motionless-
Beautiful.

Again

School time again
Books – pencils – n –
All a that
Students a movin
A comin
And goin
And goin
And all a that
Buses – n – cars
Some bicycles too
School time again
Teachers – n – students
N – parents,
A comin...
Thru.

The Trees

The trees – the trees
In the moonlight
In the starlight
Against a deep blue
Star lit sky
Is a wondrous sight
A simply
Wondrous sight
And cannot but-
Be viewed
By day
This way
But only by
The heavenly light
Of the moonlight
Starlight
Deep blue starlight sky
And...
The night.

Something

There's something in my house
That's evading me
Since my wife of
58 years left
To never return
I doze and in a chair
May sleep till morning
Comes
As if for someone or
Something to return
That never comes
And when daylight comes
And none else has
Arrived – bedtimes
Sleep time arrives.
When camping sleeping
This bothers some too
But camping sleeping usually
By 3 or 3:30 am I can do
Maybe in this house where
Where from – she left
A little over a year ago
Breaking our real here
Together of 58 years
Bothers me – it was near
Midnight too about 11:30 pm
And nearly 2 pm when
They took her away in
The van as the burial

continued

Folks plans go – that she
Left to go.
I think – I can't
Remember
But I'm almost sure
I'm reliving this in my
Mind over and over
Someway
In this house everyday
Tho I try to put those
Thoughts away
They seem to have
Remained
And I think they will
For a time – perhaps
They should.
It just may be.
I can write about them
Put them on paper
Where I can see them
Relive them with
My wife's thoughts
And when we in this way
be together
That way
and that way I think
Is good. Very good too
It does something to the
Mind more to compare– in a way
Have its way on paper-to be on paper now with her
When you lose a spouse
And a love – deep love
Of many years
A good one half

continued

Continued......Something

Of you
Disappears
And it takes a while
To level off
Fly level with the horizon
As an airplane
Must do again
I think maybe – you never
Really do again
I think one may kind
Of wobble in flight
More easily as they fly
For quite some time
Cautious – with time better
Together loves way
And that's the way
The something in my house
That's evading me
Since my wife
Of 58 years left
That near midnight – morning
Of over 1 year ago.
Seems to be –
As we communicate
Our way
Thru close distance
Tho far away
To solve this-our way
Slow gradual as-
A stream flows
Our love stream flows
To its special pace
Our pace
Loves way
That's the way I think is best
I think my wife
Agrees with me
At least
That's the way
It seems
To me.

Memories

Oh-
Beautiful memories
Are
So lovely in-
Their way
They...
Seem to brighten
Our day.

Waiting – Waiting

Roads and streets
To take one anywhere
Most anywhere
Waiting just waiting
There for you and me
On the ground- on the water
Thru the sky
Waiting, beckoning
For you and me
If we wait maybe-
We can go
If we go now
We surely go
The choice is there
For you and I
As surely as
The heavens are high
Roads and streets
To take one anywhere
Waiting there- waiting there
To take
Or- pass them by.

At Least

I must be important
At least- a little
Tho think not
Of that I be
For down here in
In the forest
Where I now be
The fog left –
A sky of sunshine
And blue
To come down
On earth to visit
A few moments
With me
I must be important
At least a little
Tho think not-
Of that, I be.

View

To view the horizon
Where the sky
Meets deep, deep water
Of the oceans waters blue
Is to view a line
As straight and level
With nary a curve
Or crook or bend
On and for endless miles
I think this straight line
Goes on forever
Where the sky meets
Ocean waters deep and blue
To where the ocean
And sky may end
At least for you
As yes me too
To view – to view.

Drifts

Summer drifts quiet
To autumn
And flowers grow on
Thru the days
Tho one flower was
Called special
To blossom another
Special way.
To blossom in memory
Forever a lovely
Spiritual way
Leaving flowers
To grow
And blossom
Their way
And love with memories
Enough for
The ageless seasons
Of
Forever.

One Morning

The doves
I heard the doves
Early – very early
One morning
Calling calling
Calling-
They kept calling
Calling...
The doves did
Their way-
Early, one morning.

Haze

The haze on the mountains
Near the ocean
But faraway
Mixed with the constant
Unending mysterious
Voice
On the ocean
Soothes a special
Way
Invites one
Just to stay
Spend the entire day
And more- on its shores
With the haze on the mountains
Near the ocean
But far away.

A Hawk

I watched a hawk
Just flying by
Hardly flapped its wings
Just soaring
Circling round and round
Very quiet
Looking on the ground
For a meal
That it could see
Little animals
On the ground
Look up around
And around
And look up in the sky
I just watched a hawk
Flying by.

One Day

As I sat on the shore
Of the ocean one day
A seagull landed
Very close to where
I sat alone – that day
The seagull walked
Quite close and looked
Me over
Stared stared intensely
Right at me
As if to say
Why, why are you
Sitting here writing
Where/I might- like to stay
I tried to speak
To the seagull my way
But the seagull looked at me
A seagull way
Stayed quite a while
And flew away- to be
With his friends not far away
Where they perhaps spoke of me
Their seagull way
As I sat on the shore
Of the ocean
One day.

Play

Put a little
Play in your day
Things go better
That way.

Thanks

The conversation
The visitation
The guitar and mandolin
Music- campfire
Singing – together´
Out under the stars
At the beach
Was beautiful-
Enjoyable-
Thanks,
For ending the day
A lovely way.

Colors

Today – the sky is blue
Soft –
Quietly, mellow
Poppy flowers
On hill sides near
Their beautiful
Yellow flowers
Wear
While the hills around
Their color display's
Of brown
To see
And the heavens above
Blend all colors with love
To make a most
Lovely day
To just
Display.

The Ocean

Go down to the ocean
Where the ocean birds stay
Where the shores are long
Where tides come go away
Where ships can be seen
In the near – and the far
Far away
Where the waters there, in its way
Can seem – to the eye
To touch the sky
The ocean speaks, at times there
In tones
Of thunder
Of silence
All alone
And of- its own
Soft to a baby's ear, sometime
Roaring, as a lion –
At other times
Go...
Down to the ocean
Where the ocean birds stay
And the ocean waters
Wait patiently
Invitingly for all
Nights and days
Also...
The ocean – the ocean
Gives comfort
There too
Living with ages
Taught it, well
Passing - thru-

The Ocean

Just Pee – in the ocean
Just pee – in the ocean
If you take a notion
Don't make commotion
The octopus won't mind
If you do – cause,
Maybe the fish
Do too.
Just pee in the ocean
Just pee in the ocean
Hey...
Maybe the whales
Do too.

Ocean Shores

Usually many
Human foot prints
And things – are
In shore sands
And near the ocean
Where people come
To hear –
The ocean and ocean life
Each person, their way
Leaving foot prints –
Foot prints
In
The ocean shore
Sands. ·

Here

I'm here,
Near the ocean
Again today
Lots of people
Are here too
I think maybe
To just see
Help
Make individual peace
Here be
And enjoy
Here
Near the ocean
Mid
Life of the ocean
A just, most
Wondrous,
Day.

This Way

He's running
He's running
He's running away
I don't think
We can catch him
When he runs that way
Thats ok...
We'll catch him
When
He's running
Again,
This way.

Bridge

Oh say...
Would you like
A
Bridge in the grass
Where you could
Walk in the grass
Cross over the bridge
And –
Walk in the grass
Again
On the
Bridge in the grass
The bridge in the grass
The bridge in the grass
The bridge in the grass.
Would you
Or say –
Could you
Like –
That,
Bridge in the grass
That,
Bridge in the grass.

To See

Its mystery – its mystery
Its mystery
And I want to see
Whats over the bridge...
There is, to see-
Why don't you,
Cross over the bridge
Cross over the bridge
And see –
The mystery
The mystery
The mystery
You want to see.

Walk

If you walk
Over the bridge
You will see
The other side
The other side
Of
The bridge
Its
Different there
If...
You walk
Over the bridge.

Hear

I hear an airplane
Flying by
I cannot see it
In the sky
It is over the clouds
And way up high
The airplane – I hear
Flying by.

Cloudy

Today is a cloudy day
The clouds
They cover the sun
Today
I cannot see
The sun today
Today is a cloudy
Day.

Still There

Late at night
When its almost morning
But the dark
Is still there to see
That's when
The spiders come out
And the mice
Walk about
Maybe raccoons
And skunks
Do too
Cats walk about
Real quiet too
Swishing their tails
Like cats
Like to
And maybe the moon
If it feels
Like it should
Might peep over
The hill
To see whats good
Late –
Late at night
When its almost morning
But the dark...
Is still there to see.

Play Today

Its hot in the sun
Real hot – in the sun
Its hot in the sun
Today
Its cool in the shade
Its cool in the shade
Its cool in the shade
Today
Lets play in the shade
Lets play in the shade
Lets play in the shade
Today
Because...
Its hot in the sun
Real hot in the sun.

Fly

I seen a bird
Fly over – a tree
And
The bird – flew away
What did you say?
I said
I seen a bird
Fly over a tree
But I'm sure
He flew
Far, far, away.

What-cha Gonna-do

Children having children
Now what-cha gonna do
Mother very young
Way under 21
Maybe 14-15-16
Sometime even 13 too
Father gone early
Left the stew.
Mother got to stay
Right up to the very
Last day
Abortion I could do
But – I,
Just didn't want to
Se I'll have a baby
Raise it by myself
At 14 yrs. Old
Can't work – too young
Still in High school
No father around
He left seems like
Long ago.
This is sure gonna be – just like mom,
Welfare for me – no other way
Sure hard to do.
This is sure gotta stop
Some way this is
Gotta stop
Maybe someday
I sure don't want it too
But maybe my baby
Will do this too
I know families that do –
I think about that
Sometime even now I do
This
Children like me
Having children
Now, what-cha gonna do.

Quarter Moon

Just a quarter moon
Tonight
But of the same light
From and in –
A full moon
In just a quarter
Moon tonight
In just a quarter
Moon tonight
A soft mysterious glow
With star lights too
With moonlight too
Flows – soft...
Beautiful, tonight.

Quiet Love

The sky is blue
Now clouds none –
Not even few,
Sunshine is here
To have its full way
If one let
That it do
To brighten clear one´s day
As the sky is blue
And let soft
Quiet love
Shine...
Just lovely –
Thru.

With Us

Those who travel
With us
On different roads
But with us
Are lovely friends
They are there – and,
Listen to us
Fill a lovely space
There too
Help us – help us
To come thru...
Those who travel
With us
On creations – different roads,
But with us
Help us every day
And help on the way.

Stirred

As soft breeze
Stirred the leaves
Moved the flowers
Refreshed –
Then... in quiet,
The breeze moved
Soft away –
To come again
Later ...
That same day.

Magnificent

They fly so fast
When they go past
And good fliers
They really are too
Maneuvering in the air
With great dexterity.
They do.
Pilots with great training
They display
For they've flown
In their lives
Many days.
Jackets of yellow
This all wear
They always do.
Jackets
Trimmed with a
Magnificent shade
Of black
Flying with precision
This they never lack
And will attack too
This you can count on
Please believe –
They will fight back
As they fly from flower
To flower
When they go past
Those yellow jacket bees
Flying, flying
Oh, so fast
When, and –
As
They go past
Always remember let them pass.

To Do

Clouds, clouds
Now that your rain
Has come
Please let the sunshine
Thru
A sky blue
Maybe a rainbow
Too.
Then on earth
Down here
We can say –
Thank you clouds
For what you do,
Your way.

Autumn

The wind
It always
Seems to know
Just when and where
It needs to blow
To bring the leaves
Just drifting
Down
When autumn
Season
Comes around

Snow

In the middle of the night
The little old lady
Came, she said
From the land of snow
Where the cold wind
Blows
In the light of day
And the dark of night
Where winters are long
And folks they freeze
And shake with their knees
Way, way, way
From the land of the snow
Where the cold wind
Blows
In the light of day
And dark of night
In middle of the night
The little old lady
Came, then – left
There she goes
Off...
To the land –
Of snow.

Where

Regina, Regina, Regina, Regina
Now where did
Regina go
If you see Regina
Please tell Regina
We all want to know
Just
Where did Regina go.

Almost Gone

Just a few
More days of summer
Summer's almost
Gone
Then Autumns here
And the leaves
Come drifting
Down
Some are
Red and yellow
Some almost
Golden brown
Just a few
More days of summer
Summer's almost
Gone.

Kind Of

When the sun
Thru the clouds
Almost
Can peep thru
And the clouds
Get sunshiny – almost
Yellowish white
Then all around
Way ,way down
On the ground
Gets nice with a
Hazy kind of
Twilight – sunlight.
It's...Quietly, warmly-
Beautifully, wonderful.

Life

They said the jury said
You killed someone
And now – we must
Kill you – and they did-
You said – the jury
It was wrong
Was later found that
You were right
The jury
It was wrong
Now what – just what
Can be done – to right the wrong
When your life they took
No one can give
For-
Its an eternal gift to live
A life no one can give
A wrong was done
Perhaps... another too
Life passes –
Life...
Passes, thru.

Cool

The clouds came
And brought
Their friend too –
The cool, the cool wind
The sun went away
And the clouds
And the wind
Made the day cool
When the sun went
Away
The clouds and their friend
Changed the day.

Someone

The building
That was here
You could see it
From every where
You could see it
From all around
Now the building
Is not here
Its not here anymore
You can see things
Not seen before
And almost right
Down into town
Because –
The building
That was here
Someone...
Took, that building
Down.

Three Bees

I see three bees
On that bush over there
And they all
Have their yellow jacket on
I guess
They must be going
To a party too
Those three bees
With their –
Pretty
Yellow jackets on.

Anyway

Fog in the morning
Room for sunshine
At noon
A nice day
Anyway.

Understand

Animals understand
I think
How we think
In a way
At least – I think
My cat does
Sometimes, some days
She seems to understand
At times
Since my wife has
Gone away
She knew the wife too
Since a kitten
In cats way.
And helps fill in
The lone some spots
In – another
Animals way
Animals,
We animals
Understand –
I think,
How we think...
In a way.

Butterflies

Little butterflies
They fly thru flowers
Little butterflies
They fly for hours
And at close of day
They fly back home
Sleep for hours
And maybe –
Dream of flowers.

Swirling Moving

Moving fog and sunshine
Swirling, moving,
Among the trees- while,
Sunshine clears
A crystal blue sky
On high
For perhaps yet
A lovely day
To pass by
Started here for me
By-
Moving fog and sunshine
In swirling motion
Among the trees – down here...
With you and me.

Calling

I hear the doves
I hear the doves
I hear the doves – a calling
They're calling who
They're calling who
They're calling you
They're calling
You...
I hear the doves
A calling
They're calling me
They're calling me
Yes can't you hear
Can't you see
I hear the doves – a calling
I hear the doves – a calling
They're calling
They're calling – they're calling.

Different

Doves seem different
From another birds
They seem like –
When they come close
If they come close
If they could,
They'd like to
Maybe...
Say a word.

In Groups

The pelicans and seagulls
Fly in groups
And explore
The ocean shores
Where they live
To see what's new – there,
For them to see
They fly round and round
As this they do
Until ...
They are thru
And then they –
Again, and again, and again
Fly in groups
And explore...
The ocean shores.

Within

To struggle – to struggle
To struggle along
To the notes
Of a far – far away song
And to climb
The mountains
Of far far away
With mist
Surrounded in mist
And heat of the day
Gives satisfaction
Not gained
Without struggle
For struggle –
Gives appreciation
Of love ...
From
Within.

Away

Tonight is the only
Night that belongs
To the day
That has just
Passed away
For tomorrow
Will be – another
Day
You can see it
If ...
You're given
That day,
And – it will have
Its own tonight
But this,
Tonight – belonged,
To the day
That just – passed
Away.

People

People have houses
They have tents
Too
And sometime
People love too
Go camping
Live outside
In tents too
Then ...
Go back to –
Their house,
People,
Some people –
Do this ,
They do.

Sometime

Understand – understand
Sometime
Its difficult to
Understand – understand
Its like...
Talking to a fish
Who lives in the water
About you
Living and breathing
On land
Maybe the fish
Would not
Understand – understand
How you – could
Live on land- live on land
Not in the water
Live on land – live on land
But...
You do – you do
Sometime – its
Just difficult, to ...
Understand – understand.

Passing Thru

For some things
In life
One has to do
There's no book
To instruct
On how to do
Its different in life
Each one goes thru
In how life offers
The things
We must
Go thru
And how we handle them
As we go thru
Its quite different
For each one – to each one
Passing thru
Lots in life changes early
Late – most or more
More it seems – late in life
Passing thru
Effecting each one different
As it happens – handled different
By each with, no instructions – passing thru.

Birds

Ocean birds – ocean birds
Near the ocean
There's ocean birds
They like the ocean
Other birds – I see not,
On these shores –
Only ocean birds
I see
These shores...
Explore.

Quietly

Quietly listen
when other's
are speaking
to you.
One can learn
much-
When this
you do.
Listen quietly
Don't say-a word
Listen-Listen
Then, they
will be heard.

Early Years

After the early years
of marriage
and small things
are
talked and smooth,
worked out.
Then the two
can consider most
settling
together is
done.
The two can
then become, as one
after the early years
are done.

Mysterious

The sky is dark
and deep of blue
The moon is half
most halfway thru
The stars around
all shine tonight
Also...
The moon and stars
Light earth
with soft,
mysterious - moon
and starlight, while...
The sky - is dark.
mid,
Deep of blue.

Evening

The sky is clear
and crystal blue
The evening's coming
and pretty soon
too
soon the stars
and harvest moon
will be shining
way up high
in the night time
sky,
Day time has
only a very few hours
more to stay
because-
evenings on its way
the sky is crystal blue
and evenings coming
pretty soon
too.

The Life

The soft falling of raindrops
causes fields of crops
green of grass, trees
to grow
Long after the rain
has ceased to be
The good, the love
it gave - counting on
in memory - in ways
which are, lovely,
beautiful, spiritual
eternal.
And the life of a rainfall
all god given life is good,
remembered - in love
never forgotten
as the years pass, on, on
and on, on, on - into...
Eternities.

Comfortable

When you're older
over 40
This you do
you will find
it comfortable too
Put shoulders forward
hands together
held in back
stomach down
Toward the ground
That's the way
you walk around
When you're older
if
This you do
You will find it
comfortable - natural
too.
You old gaz - zoo,
when you're older.

Waiting

To wait makes -
you
Slow down,
To a crawl
in a way
and think - and act
as perhaps
You should
at times...
Thru - out
The day.
Waiting - waiting
Quietly
Quietly... has its way.

Choice

Back from camping
Sun's still shining too
Quite a lot of today's
left -
What's there to do.
Just finished a rice bowl
at Jack in the Box
Go home now - unload the Van
Do what possible I can
to finish the day
A positive way
To not feel boxed in
as rice in a bowl
with a lid on top
for the rice inside with a top
in place.
Must account for each grain
in the bowl
under the top covering the bowl
Back from camp I must be free
To do my way, my choice
for the rest of the day
tomorrow too
That's my way - I must say
with...
Quite a lot of today - still left
before today's thru back from camping too.

Animals

Tigers and Lions
eat animals
Humans eat
animals too
Humans cook
animals before
eating them
Lions and tigers
eat them
as they are
still its
animals eating
animals.
What's the menu
Today?
Lions, tigers
or humans
choosing
What's the menu
today?

Curtain

The motionless
curtain
standing and still
Till touched
by you - now...
it swings
and
swings
To tell you
Thanks
and tell you
Hi,
for touching
it
as you -
passed by.

The Way

Help, help, help
others
Don't forget about
little old you
Help you - Little old you
along the way
some too.
Then you can better
help others
along the way
But be fair
along the way
help others
and you-too,
on the way
there.
Help - help - help
Help - two - three - four
Help.

Noisy

Cell phones now
makes it
even in quiet places
so you have
To listen
To people talking
What they're saying
They seem to talk loud
Just loud as can be
so folks hear -
and you see
Those cell phones
The phones are
helpful - good
but folks are noisy...
Noisy, noisy, just,
as noisy as can be.

A Car

Want a new car
but the old one
has the memories
memories, memories
memories of long ago
The new one has
To start a new
To make memories
memories, memories
now that I don't
use the auto much
and no ones here
except myself
The old cars like
a friend -
That knows my touch
and offers much
plus memories too
it kind of helps
The days pass thru.
But still it's getting
old with parts
that soon may
part - so I must
decide on
an auto
new
start
new
Memories– all,
new
someway
they'll
build
as days.
They will
They'll
fit in
too.

For Today

People come in
all sizes - all types
I see em in this room
Where I now stay
This day
There's -
fat, small, skinny tall
short, that's me
Ball headed
some, hair headed
slender - not so slender
old, young,
middle aged too
smiling, frowning
What have you
Nationalities too
Take your pick
People's there for you
Same way - same size
Same type
Interesting too
Peoples here to stay
at least for today.

Dressed

When folks come in
all dressed
in suits with fancy shirts
and fancy ties
it makes them look
important, at least then.
If others are dressed
as workers then.
But the folks
all dressed with
Suits and ties
we never know
how they pass-
Time, by.

Stay

Chairs
We sit on them
we stand on them
We push them around
We shove them.
Pile junk on them
Do almost any thing
conceivable
to them
and...
They support and
stay with us.
Chairs,
chairs are very -
good friends.

Duty

On jury duty today
sitting in a room
Just passing time away
waiting to be called
To listen to the courts
decision
of a Jury's opinion
The Jury's way.
On Jury today
Yes, waiting to be picked
To make a decision
in a
Jury's way.
A citizens duty...
done, the proper-
way.

A Record

A note is a record
of time gone by
That shows how time
and moments
doth fly
Also showing
how notes can
in a way
keep as record
in a slight
Teenk-see-weenk-see
Bit
or slight sliver
of that second
silent moment
of
wonderful
kindly beautiful
Time
This imagery... of,
These, notes.

Lifetime

Once one leaves
If you're old enough
to remember
They're part of you
as when you first met
They're still life time
member's.
The place they passed
The funeral home
The place they rest
Its part of you
all the way thru
accompanies you
in a very special way
In kind of a protective
Loving way.
Once one leaves
If you/re old enough
To remember
They're still a lifetime
member.

To You

There are things
in life - some good - some bad
That happen to you
you may never know
Just why
They happen to you
But they do
You must just
go on
keep on - movin
movin thru
This you must do
Just keep on movin
movin thru
its all in the plan
maybe cause you can
When these thing in life
some good - some bad
they happen
happen to you
and they do.

If

If, that of
bad
good can be done
If, that of
good
bad can be done
maybe - just maybe
an understanding
of love…
someway
can come thru -
just maybe
and…
If.

Snow

Snow snow…
There is no snow
Right here -
There is no snow
there is no snow here
we brought
it here
on the hill - look,
there is snow.
The sun is hot
And birds watch too
For before perhaps…
Maybe - snow…
They've seen none
and -
They will watch
Till the snow
is thru.
See there is snow here
and children bring -
bring shovels
toys and things
to play - people.
Play in the snow,
There is snow here-cause,
We brought it here-for children to play in.

Today

Children playing
windy too
A lot of sunshine
blue sky too
Thanksgiving's finished
and after today
Novembers thru.
But today – is nice
A lovely day today
Because…
Children are playing
its windy,
with
A lot of sunshine-Holiday love,
also -
Blue sky too.

Others

To help others
one may come,
as one to be -
helped,
in ways of some.
And we behold
Them not
We but see
substance of
of them being sent
or we see the
substance not-they help silently and leave
Helping others in need
is beautiful
if
responsibility
as a steward
of love
thru others
quite like
sky of blue
lets and helps
love shine
thru
by helping all
and others
helps love,
flow thru.

White Streak

A snow white
streak
I see in the cold cold sky
and its - coming
from the hot air
of
A jet airplane
flying far
going by -
in our
big,
deep blue sky.

Wrote

My friend he wrote
a book
wrote he
He wrote about
his family
about when he was
in the Army
In - fan - try
and when he
traveled over to
German-ny
France and I think
The Nether Lands
Japan, Korea, Vietnam
many places
my friend
from memory
remembered
as he wrote
this book
he wrote, wrote he.

Water Wheels

Pour water
on the water wheels
Pour water
on the water wheels
pour water
on the water wheels
The wheels
Turn very fast
more water
water, water, water
Children, pour water
water, water, water
more water
water, water, water
make the wheels - turn fast.

Raceway

I heard some autos close
They sounded far away
Their engines running
wildly
And shifting gears
their way
But when I thought
must be in preparation
for something
coming here soon
Because -
I'm camping on
The Laguna raceway
and to hear auto's
speeding here
that's ok.
There's lots and lots
of raceway
speeding room.

No clouds

Clouds, Clouds
There are no clouds
No clouds
In the sky today
only blue sky
sunshine
in the sky
today
and the sun
is far
far away
Clouds, Clouds
There are no clouds
no clouds
in the sky today.

One Bird

One little bird
I see
sitting alone
In a great
big tree.
Looking to see
I think -
everything,
one little bird can see.
By looking close-
At all one, little bird
can see.
Sitting alone -
in a great
big tree.

Morning Early

When its early - in the morning
and the moon is shining
and the stars are too
and you're out - and you're camping
there's no one, but you
you see lights of a town
in a valley below
you feel lonesome
But they are there
and here's you
They don't know you
you don't   know them
But here you are - and,
you are a friend - that way.
Its not so lonesome then
When its early in the morning
and the moon is shining
and the stars, are too.

A Place

Tractors, steam shovels
Caterpillars too
There's a place
for the shovel -
The man with the shovel
He still
has work
There is still work
he can do
That the tractor's
steam shovels
and caterpillars
can't do…
But…
The man with
The shovel,
His jobs
Now…
They are few.

The Calf

Swing that lasso
Swing it high
Loop it round
The calf a running by
Stop your horse
While you jump down
To do what
cowboys do,
While your horse
stands a watching you
flipping the calf
tyin the calf
and doin it
Fast
Tight
and right
for the range
or the
Rodeo.

Of December

Its the month
of December
and 4 pm hour
of the day.
I must get
out of bed
before the day
slips always
its the month
of December
And dark always
remembers -
to come early…
December days.

Slide

Thanksgiving passed
Christmas soon
Then -
A new year too
Another year slipped by
Passed swiftly
quietly - thunderously
smooth, right thru.
strange…
But in a way - day's
when grouped together
like years are.
Kind of - do what
In a way… their way
That way - years go…
Kind of like - winds blow.
And like, now,
Thanksgiving's passed
Christmas soon - new years too
years slip
slide, soft, soft, softly…thru.
right thru.

Almost

This year is almost
gone
This year is almost
past
in 3 more days
The new year is here
with a lot of new things
We all must share
some good - some bad
The futures given
That way
good or bad.
This year is almost
past
leaving some - taken some
But tip toeing by
quiet-n-noisy
but...
fast.

Run

When you're just - age 3 or 4
you run, run, run
sometime
really, really fast
where are you going? maybe you
don't know - most times
you just run, run, run
because its fun
its fun, to run
when you're just
Age 3 or 4
or, sometime more.

People Do

Quite strange - in a way,
to be,
inside, inside
when its cold
outside, outside
when its hot
where we'll be
(maybe)
will usually be
Whether its cold
or hot... or not.
That's what people do
because work
They have too
Still quite strange
in a way
but has to be-where we be.

Quiet

So quiet, so quiet
are the hawks
in the sky
as they float, float
in the air
looking for a meal
on the ground
below
as they quietly
float
by in the sky.
Look out, look out, little animals...
on the ground
below
The hawks
floating
so quiet- so quiet
so quiet
in the sky.
Soaring, soaring - looking for, "maybe you"... as
they
pass by.

Turkeys

Now lets see,
Thanksgiving Day is coming
prepare the pumpkins
Squash, sweet potatoes
ripe apples
and
pears too.
But turkeys -
You better stay away
Till after, thanksgiving day
If you know what's good
for you
Stay away Christmas Day
New years day too
maybe come back about
Easter time
That's a pretty safe time for you
But...
You better stay away
On - Thanksgiving day.

The Season

Some flowers bloom
even when
Snow begins to fall
They bloom late
in the season
That is their season
That is their reason
for and to bloom.
In the autumn
In the winter
blooms may flourish
and appear
If we permit
Them to
come forth -
with their brilliance
shining thru.
In the autumn
in the winter
or even...
When the snow falls -
too.

A Speck

"Hey"-
There's a speck
In our big sky of blue
Oh - its just
and airplane
flying thru
say airplane -
Way up high in the sky
Where the sun and moon
pass by
Don't you bump into
a star
In our big sky of blue
as you
fly thru.

Passin - Thru

An afternoon - and
a sunny one too
Where the sky is blue
With few clouds
on high
Just drifting by
to make a quiet
afternoon
Just almost lazy, lazy,
almost just perfect
"But", for a really, really
perfect day
I'd want a rainbow too
while clouds - be few
And with the sunny
afternoon, tho-
The few of clouds
Quiet, real quite
Like it is.
I'm still gonna call it
a
Lazy, lazy afternoon.
Thats what - I'll do
While it's...
Passin thru.

137

Never

Your shadow
in a picture
always
poses with you
stays with you
never - leaves you,
is always with you
your shadow - your shadow
That's in a picture.

One

When living
In a home
of
only one,
Leaving some
undone
gives one
feeling,
of -
Not just one.
That another
may come
sometime
to clean.
All cleaned
gives a feeling
All is finished
no one will come
all is ok.
This kind of,
comes into play - unconsciously
when one lives
in a home
of one.

The Way

So lovely to see the sunrays
That mark a sky at dawn
and seem to say - Hi - I am with you
all the way along, this day
Tho we may separate - along the way
We never are lost - Tho we may stray
For like love that binds
The far off stars
To gather near at twilight - evening - night
The sunrays that marked
The sky at dawn
Remains with you all thru memories
in love thru out the night
each night,
Till sunrays lights the sky
again each day
at dawn.

Thoughts

After Christmas
ones world - in a way
starts the next day
in thoughts
quite same.
But in another way
The thoughts of -
Christmas, visitors, shopping
Presents- holiday- rushing
The unknown
much…
Kind of relaxed
sort of feeling
After Christmas
Ones world in a way
kind of almost
Just a wee little - slips back to
Ones before Christmas days
holidays-their way
of course now, and soon coming
There's still -
New year's, preparation, to do
After Christmas- Is thru.

With Time

There's an old person
and like the sun
From dawn till noon
noon to twilight
evening then the night
have their run - with slight
but little change
in what they do
as they pass thru.
They understand
most all we do.
And are quite wise, in what they do
For most have done
What we now do - They have done too,
that old person like the sun
passing thru, on this run
Which we all - with time, must do
Aging as slowly
as we do…
with time-to be, old.

The Life

The soft falling of raindrops
causes fields of crops
green of grass, trees
much, to grow.
Long after the rain
has ceased to be
The good, The love
It gave - continues on
In memory - in ways
Which are lovely
beautiful, spiritual
Eternal.
And the life of a rainfall
all god given life
is good
is remembered - in love
never forgotten
as the years, pass -
on, on - and on,
Into…
Eternities.

Out West

Lasso's and cowboys
cowgirls too
Horses and cows
Little calves too
Sheep and goats - baby sheep too
saddles and wagons
Rattlesnakes that crawl by
with a lizard or two.
Sleeping bag, a pan -
To cook with and fry.
And a good rifle and pistol
That shoots far and high
Of course now a days
a pickup and trailer
is all part of the make-up's
of cowboys, cowgirls,
and cowhands you 'll find
in searching the stretches
of far- far… way-
way out west.

Passing Thru

The holiday season's
Passing thru
Thanksgiving, Christmas
new year.
The civilized devouring
animal's- fowl
all holiday thru
vegetarians tho,
Permitting animals, fowl
to thrive, survive.
Stores love
holidays for
families to enjoy and,
The celebration-togetherness
Tinsel
and all-about life
As the holiday season
passes-
Shimmering, Thru.

Can Be

Happy, happy - folks can be
changed
when something's happened
They can see
To them
It seems to stay
and be
enough - to make
Them never forget - the past.
Then they
seem
To always be alone
and inside kind of turn-
Turn to stone
from what they
Long, long ago did see.
This…
Sometime happens
even-to
Happy, Happy folks
This - can be.

Your Path

Twilight glow mid setting sun
and cool the hours of evening
Beautiful the rising sun
That shines with love
o'er night that's done
then starts the day -light on its
golden way
with light on pathes
seen, unseen
A guiding way
And as your path - guides you.
May twilight love that glows,
as the setting sun
yet beautiful
with rays that extend forever
as the rising sun
shine on your path
with everlastingly beautiful
spiritual, guiding light-
Forever… and ever.

A Nitch

There's a nitch
in life
and you may fit
there too.
Now that nitch
be filled
that's
swell too
if you fit
in the notch
and the notch
of your fit-in life
is ok.
Then the notch
in -
life will
be filled. (Maybe)-if life ok's.

Can Do

The spoils the treasures
The diamonds too
They shine thru
The treasures
The diamonds do
They make history
They really do
As life shines
Thru
The spoils
And
That life
Can do.

Strange

The brain- the brain
can some time
do strange things
An accident
can happen
To some one-
very close - far
miles far away
and the mind of
miles far away
understands
and knows the time
of the accident
the brain- the brain
can sometime
do strange things.

The There - The Hear

I hear voices
and there's no one there
I talk to you
and you don't hear
You talk to me
We look- we see
I think, you think
Folks aren't there
You are here
I am here
Something's wrong
What is wrong?
The there- The hear
The song - I hear- Oh that music
Tho strange to me
No one can see - The what I see
Nor can they hear
They think I imagine
But I hear - I feel
This strange to me
I hear…
and there's no one there-tis imagination I'm sure
must be. Maybe.

Thru

Laws of a land
which excludes
The creators laws
of the land
will crumble from
the land
The consumers discard
Them as rising
Powers be.
Consistency
creators laws
of all consistency
must be.
A basic standard
for all to be
must be.
And to include
Laws of land
The creators laws
for all - of -
honest and true
leads and brings
all with love
in the creators
creations…
of - time
lovely
Thru.

All

No matter
The size problem
Whether good, bad
Large or small
Have faith…
The creator
Is there to
Silently help-
With help - thru,
It all.

Debt

If possible
make possible
To owe no other
except for love
If debt is owed
The soul is too
If none is owed
others will come
to you
for help - to help
Thru
Owe none other
except for love
and love - is free
as the wind - sun,
moon stars
They
are free. If possible...
Make this possible.

Wondrous Way

Every day any day
is a beautiful- just,
lovely day
and is given in a
wondrous way
with love
from the creator
and its given
in seconds, minutes
hours
for each to discover
in their-individual
ways
To best use the
given day
In a individual
and should be a
Lovely, eternal way
Every day and any day.

When It Happens

When to others
It happens too
its hard to see
the way
They see- things thru
But when -its you
Things happen to
Things you can-
more see
what they seen
and realize what
new
you, see-
in what you see
of the hard
To see.
When it happens…
To you-for you-
to see thru.

Amazed

In phase out of phase
Lights of colors
moving shapes
crafts seen too
All does seem of strange
Thru
In phase out of phase
I'm amazingly
amazed - what,
a little known-
of the unknown
can do,
In phase, out of phase.

Wonders

How wonderful
and beautiful too
The wonders of
each day
comes lovely in
its way too
Thru
sunshine, clouds
The cloudy - Twilight
Evenings, nights
Enlightens…
How wonderful
and beautiful -
The wonders of
each day.

Stay

As we stay
In one place
longer and longer
The things we accumulate
all piled up,
gets higher and higher
as we get -
older and older
This happens to
young middle aged
old folks too-
How about you?
How many things
do you have
you don't really need
As you stay and stay
and stay,
Has this happened
to you?

Listen

Stop talking
And listen
from the mouth
comes
good and evil
words to say
Stop talking and listen
Ask…
Let the creator
Tell you
Tell you quietly -
Quietly
What to say
Stop talking
Stop talking
Stop- talking
and- just… Listen.

Morning

Each morning
is a miracle
given new, and
everyday
Each noon, twilight
and evening
we see are miracles
too
But each morning
is a miracle
given new by
the creator
To all- at dawn
and start
of day
every day...each
Morning, morning.

143

Decisions

Decisions - Decisions
must be made
everyday
Whether you feel
good or bad
They must be made
everyday.
And then you leave
at the end
of the day
to feel good
or bad
or only - half way
with all the
decisions- decisions
you made for
the day.

To Start

The longest walk -
of many miles with a single
step did start
The longest day - with
first ray of dawn
did start
The many miles of a
lengthy journey with
The first mile must start
The longest battle of
many battles - with
The first battle, must start
The large
The most enormous
of all
must… at start
be small
like small
of all
to start.

Hallway

Oh yes…
On the way - you'll pass,
The magic hallway
going there
with many doors-
To open
each door opened
will have much new
To see… you-
never before, did see
That's new for you
To see
On the way, your way
The magic hallway
Oh yes-
The magic, hallway
to there.

Away

Saturday night
Just slipped away
At 12pm
It went in its way.
I was sitting here too
Now its nearly 4am
Sunday morning
Saturday night's thru
Just slipped away
Not a word did it say
Gosh-what a way to
End a day
Saturday night-
Just slipped a way.

That Way

The world is very funny
one doesn't need lots of money
To be happy in the world
All is required - is this -
Do something that is honest
something that is good
Help those you meet in need
and loved ones too
Do what you think
is the best in you
and others will respond
in this way too
Then in this way
Happiness will shine
slowly… Thru
To you
If one doesn't
contribute
to the world
something
acceptable
in a way.
The world
will dispose
of you
in some way
The world is funny - in that way too
you will find this to be true.

One more time

Yer bloods a bilin
Hearts a beatin fast
Waitin just a waitin
Horse in the chute
Calfs in the chute
A waitin-just a waitin
Don't wanna go to quick
Don't wanna lose points
Gotta time it just right
Hearts a beatin fast stirrups ready
Now's the time we're off
Come on arm cum-on cum.on
Flip that lasso
Ah ha aaa got I'm
Got that calf
Got I'm round the neck
Flipped the rope
Tied it fast round the saddle horn
Now off quick, quick, quick
Good-good-good
Steady steady, steady boy
Hold that calf
He's sure a jumpin
Gotta get im quick.
Got I'm
Now to flip I'm
Good done it
Flipped I'm
Got eese legs
Just right

continued

continues ...One More Time

2 fronts pushed together one back
Tween the front
Now to tie all four
Hold em together
Got the leather
Twixt muh teeth
Yank the leather
Tied those legs
Done it all
Timing was good
Timing was real good
What a day
One more time
Beautiful-beautiful
Somebody likes me
Just like back in corpus christi
I got one more rodeo time
Sure felt good.

Play

The sun is shining
The sky is blue
Tho clouds they corer.
Some blue sky too
And children play,
They play here too
Because...
The clouds let
Blue of sky
With sunshine...
Thru.

Flower

From a seed – a flower
Lovely did grow
In a field of many
It did grow
Another flower grew
In a field – not far away
These flowers met
Produced seeds
Others flowers grew
Together happy for years
Then one flower
Faded away
The other flower – wilting slightly
Remained for years
After faded too
In memory...these flowers
Their flowers
All flowers of creation
The creator grows
With love
Will be remembered
In memories
Eternally – spiritually
And.
Forever.

The Life

The soft falling of raindrops
Causes fields of crops
Green of grass, trees
Much, to grow.
Long after the rain
Has ceased to be
The good, the love
It gave- continues on
In memory- in ways
Which are lovely
Beautiful, spiritual
Eternal
And the life of a rainfall
All god given life
Is good
Is remembered- in love
Never forgotten
As the years, pass-
On, on- and on,
Into...
Eternities.

You

Your promise
Of good
To do good
Is you
Make your promise
True
Your promise
Is you.

The Season

Christmas comes
Like any other day
And then it goes
On its way
Maybe its the music
Or
Because the season
Is long
Or
Maybe
Its the reason
Of the season
As Christmas
Moves along
It always
Is different
Than other
Holidays.
Because Christmas
Leaves and gives
A feeling
Of a special
Kind of love- that's different,
When Christmas
Un like any other day- leaves...
And then goes
On its way-maybe it's the reason,
of the day.

Words

From stories
The minds seen
The hearts felt
That hurry
To be written-and,silently
unfold
before old-retold, come
Many words.

Leaves

It's spring time and
Oh look
The leaves are
On my tree today
They were not on my tree yesterday
They must have come
Quiet like day light
Leaves the sky
After sunset
The leaves are beautiful
I love the leaves
Oh look…
The leaves green leaves
Are on my tree
Today
And…
It's spring time.

Do

Folks may talk-what they will do,
But you never
Really know
What you really
Will do
Until
You have to do
What you
Really- really
Have to do
Ne matter
What folks
May say
That they will do.

Till dawn

Afternoon
Morning- ebbed
Away
Twilight, evening
Night
Tip toes in
Another day
Waned
Away
In a, soft
Quiet
Ancient
Age less- way.
Till dawn
Of...
Another, day.

Some…

Cowboy- cowgirls
Out west- needs.
Lasso's for cowboys
Cowgirls too (good saddle bridle)
Horses and cows, some-
Little calves too
Sheep and goats
Baby sheep goats too
Saddles and wagons (good harness too)
Rattle snakes that crawl by
With a lizzard or two. (to shoot at)
Sleeping bags
A good pan with which
To cook or fry.
And a good rifle
And pistol that can shoot far and high
Of course now a days
A pick up and trailer
Is now also- a part of...
A cowboys, and cowgirls needs
When you're way out west
And you may need more- if you ain't too poor.

Another Day

Today was just
Another day
After tonight
Came along- its way
And
Tomorrow too
Will be
Just another day
When tomorrow night
Comes thru.
The days, the nights
Weeks, months, years
make
Age flow in.

So, thru it all, we...
Can just remember
That...
Today was just
Another day
And tomorrow too
Will be,
Just another day.

Ask

Never forget to ask
Of all- To do, something-
They can easy do.
No matter how big
Or small they be
If they can it do
Easily,
For...all-
Like to feel
Important, they do.
As they
This way-
Pass thru.

Dark of Night

After twilight soon
Comes,
The dark of night
Each day
Near Christmas time.
For soon a new year
Tip toes in- on feet of quiet
Making short- the light
Of day.
Soon after new year
Tho
Dark of night, after twilight
Comes not so soon,
Each day.
Making longer the light
Of day- . each day
Till about Christmas
And new years
Time...
Each year.

Cats Way

Cats sleep- sleep
Lots in the day
And in mornings
Early hours
They like to,
Go every where
And look at all
They can see
There. In the dark...
Then come back
In
Mornings
Early hours
Sleep- sleep
Lots in the day.
That's
Cats way
Cats like-
That way.

Bicycles

2 bicycles I see,
Off they go
Off they go
With blinking
Lights of blue
Off in to night
With their riders
Rolling rolling
Merrily
As the darkness- round them
Grows
2 bicycles
Off off off
In to the dark
Of night
They go off they go.
Rolling- rolling
Rolling
Off- off- off
They go.

Baptized

If
One believes
Deep within
The creator
Is true
Be baptized
By water and
Still believe
Deep within
Love
Of the creator
Is true.
The baptism
Of the love
And faith
Of ones
Faith and love
Of the creator have begun, and
Life starts then their journey
Eternally
Thru.

Music Can

Music can take you
If you let it
To places- where,
You're been
Places
You might be
Going to
Or
Leave you
Just
Where you are
If
You let it
Or
You can ignore
It
And let it
Just like that- be.
.music can take you
Music can
Lots do.
And...
for free.

Helping

Excuse me
I've been so busy
Talking of helping
Others
Just overlooked
The fact
That you...myself-
Really need
Help too,
Excuse me
Please.

Wise

Fix neat in place
The place
Where you awaken
Each night,
Or
Day.
And it will
Help to
Organize the
Day- that
You must usc.
That is your day
By helping
Organize at,
Awake...
Is wise.

Swallowed

Cause half a sleep
Course i'll never
Really know
But think i swallowed
A bug
Some kind of insect
A fly, a spider
A caterpillar
Hope not a slug
I remember
It tasted- kind of
Sweet
Course...
I'll never really know
What it really was
Cause I was half
A sleep.
Hope it wasn't a
Spider a caterpillar
Or even...
A slug- gosh.

Is Lovely

Communication
Is lovely
In its
Many many ways
Of talking
And listening
.Too
Even in silence
Communication's
There too
Speaks loudly if
We permit it to Communicate
Is lovely helpful,
Beautiful too
In its
Many many
Ways- daily, for use.

Told

Children believe
In their home
What they are told
And as they- grow old
They believe
And do,
More and more
In their homes
What they see, think
And most
Of
What they, were told.

To Do

To have a war
That never stops
Cost a lot of
Money too
¨this¨most any group
Of folks can do.
To make an auto
That never stops
Keep, running never
Breaks down
Anytime
Or an airplane
Ship, or train
This now this
Is difficult to do
Now this no one
Has yet, been able,
To do.
But...
To have a war
That never stops
Is quite in fact,
Very easy to do.
And... lots of folks do.

Away

Once passed away
You're gone to stay
Never to come back
Again
This way.
kept…
In others mind
Sometime, lifetimes.

More

Two hurts together
Make hurt
Hurt
More
Two mourners
Together
Make mourning
Much more
Two sugars
Poured together
Fills a container
Fast more
More of
Most any thing
Makes
More, more
And...especially more hurt. Does.

Gone Away

Gone one year
Gone away- to stay
Missed one year
Seems right to the day
Gone two years
Gone away- to stay
Missed 4 years
Seems right to the day.
Maybe this missing
A loved one- gone away
Away to stay
Will not double in time
As now seems, now-
That they're left- gone away
But settles to the time
And time and the mind
Will be more kind, to– remember then,
Pass years- pass time.

A Holdin' On

Steady old bull
Steady old bull
Yer sure a rarin
Gotta remember
I'm on my own here
I've done it all
Least i think i have
Old bulls sure a rarin
Any second now
We'll be out there
The ropes round
This critters belly
Tightened it my self
Holdin it tight
Other hands in the air
Can't leave I'm now
You know.
Don't wanna lose points
Gotta ride I'm
Gotta hold on tight
Can't let I'm flip fall on me
Like before- course was
Only 16 then long time ago
Am now better, now.
Things er sure goin thru
Muh brain today.
I'm a holdin on
We're ready
Ain't we bull
Hey chutes open we're off
Cum on bull do yer thing bull
I'm ready yer not gonna flip me
Gonna stay those 8 seconds
Er sure gonna try.
These second ur

Goin fast
Gotta hang on
Gotta make it
Guys said this un
Had been rode twice
Before
Sure is a tough critter
Aw gosh he flipped me
But think I made
The seconds in
Got my points
Landed good
"move" "move" get outta here
Quick bulls sure a comin
He's a real mean critter
And ul stomp and gore yuh
I'm outta here
Thanks clowns
Take I'm away
Listen to that crowd
Sure been a nice day
And...
Another time
Another lovely time
Thanks
Thanks again
You're sure
Good to me.
Oh look at that young
Lady gitten ready
To ride the barrels
She's sure a pretty one
That's a beautiful horse
She's a ridin too
Sure hope she makes it
Good luck lady
Un bye.

continued

Season

The season- of the now
We see
And the way it comes
To us
Wherever we may be
So beautifully
In memories-
With young and old
Also
In gifts of
Eternal lively
Very own
And
Equally blended
Thru
The season of the now
We see
This beautiful
Christmas season
The lovely Christmas eve
Right now
A beautiful and
Eternal Christmas
Soon- very blessed
Blending smoothly
In silence
As sun, moon, stars.
And comes to each
With a special
Very special blessing
Felt within...
Thru the creators
Love
The season of the now
We see,
Christmas…
Merry Christmas
And, with-
Happy new year. Is almost here.

Each Day

Start from the heart
Each day
Deep deep within
Each day
The heart guides
From within
Each day the right path
To be in each day.
And should be
Considered, carefully
With deep thought.

Ways

When peace leaves
And hate comes
With hateful ways
Peace thru love
Can return
With loving ways
And again bring
Peace,
Hate will leave
Taking its
Hateful ways
And peace returns
With peaceful
Ways.

A Love

After losing a love
Seems a year goes by
Similar to a bird on high
Passes- in silence
From the blast
Of
Wind in the sky.
And a second year
With the time of a year goes by
And now- too
With years passing
After losing a love
Seems years just goes by
My my
How years
Years seem to fly.

Light

A light in dark
Gives light
For one to step
By light- in dark.
And...
When the light's
At rest
One can rest
Be still...
Then step again
In dark,
With light
From light.

That Way

Sometime.
The days
Just go that way
Just take
Your choice
And rejoice.
Sometime
The days
Just go...
That way.

On the Hills

The sunshine
On the hills today
Thru clouds on the hills
Seen from far away
Made a lovely sight
Under a cloudy blue sky
That I viewed
From far, far away
As sunshine
Shined...shaded,
On the hills- today…and was just-
Majestically, beautiful.

Soup

With cold weather
Hot soup
With Christmas
And
New years passing thru
Now that was- just
A most...
Delicious something
To do, and
With a magic touch
Thank you
Thank you very much.

Christmas Tree

From an old
Piece
Of masonite
A little, teeney
Christmas tree
I made for me
For Christmas
After you left
On April 15,2010
And it served
For me
My Christmas tree
I keep it in
A cabinet too
My Christmas tree
My little teeney
Masonite Christmas tree
And...
I'll always feel
You were- with me
Thru...
That Christmas,
Christmas 2010
And that you'll always be
In a way- with me.

Language

Clicks in your language, for some-
Tells us- your
Language, is...
From long long ago
Interesting, interesting
How lives and living goes
Languages, languages
Tell us of long long
Ago.
Isn't that beautifully
Beautifully nice
A very nice
Thing to know
Just to know
How far- very far back
A click ,a spoken sound
In a language, in years
Can go.

Old Year

With so many holidays
And good days too
All year thru (the old year)
When new years eve
Like it is today
Comes real- soft like
Quiet thru
The old year
Takes
A long holiday
With good days
And never comes
Back this way
When its days
Are
Thru.

Drew

She drew a picture
Of that little girl
She drew a picture
Of Mary too
And then what did
She do?
She said she had
To leave
But today that lady
Drew a lot of pictures
A beautiful way
She just
Drew and drew
And drew away today.

Worst Enemy

Most of the time
And to just be kind...to,
The worst enemy
One can have
Is you
You tell yourself
I can't do this
You tell yourself
I can't do that
Then you don't even try
To do this
Or that
You pass yourself
Right by
Not even small
Don't try
When you could just easy do
Most what you. Just try to do
Really...
Most of the time just to be kind...to,
The worst enemy one can have
Is you.

All Way Thru

Muddy sand water mud, now that's
Children's study– also,
Swings and things like them, like them
To learn to play from too– by,
Children's rules.
For play
Real, real, play you know
Children enjoy
Children's rules
For children play
An apple, an apple
Learn an apple
Taste an apple
What it is what it really is
Then describe it fully
Put it in your memories
School.
Muddy, muddy
Children's study make memories
To build to cherish
All way
Thru.

Rocking

An old metal
Rocking chair
Outside
Seen it just
Rocking in the wind.
Nobody sitting
On the chair within
It was just rocking
To and fro
An old rocking chair
With human ghostly
Familiar within, unseen-
Just rocking, rocking
Silently rocking...
Rocking
Rocking in the wind.

Quietly Quiet

The quietly quiet
Of quiet
Right after midnight
Hours right
After midnight
Seem to have a way
Of speeding hours
For soon after midnight
Comes dawn
Bringing, light
Of day.

Me

Of all the enemies
I can see
The worst… I think
Is me
Of all the friends
That I can see
The best– I think
Is me
Who is me?
If I look deep deep
Really deep inside
The really me is there
For me and then
Most times I doubt
That me
Of all the enemies
I can see
Is my friend and enemy
Me.

Far

On a hill
The light can be seen
From far
Like the light
Of a far off star
Which all can see
Without trouble
So free
And be
Enlightened
By the city
On a hill
Like a star
Star light…
In the heavens
Off far.

Must Have Faith

One must have faith
Must have faith
To have belief
One must have faith
To have trust
Must have trust
Must have trust
It is a must
One must have faith
And trust
To have belief
Belief in God,
True belief.

Something

Poetry- exists...in
What one see's
In the day- night- evening
Noon, anytime
In each given 24 hour's
That gives an imagery
For one to write about
The right words to
Put out
To paint an image
In words
To come differently
Tho same to each
In words
But have a meaning
Of something seen
A picture of something
In mind that could
Be made- thru thinking.
To wonder about
That exists some where
Or.
Round about
A poem- this can do
Can
Silently carry you
Near- far- or...
Right close by
Thru words, seen by the eye
Or heard
In some way
What the poem had to say
In its own
Personal way.
Different, but the same
Of something
About something
Seen
In
Poetry's
Way
Where,
Poetry always,
Exists.

While Camping

I had just a
Splendoriously
Wonderful time
While camping
Most everything
Happened as I wanted it
To
The birds flew quiet
And free was the wind
sunshine too and
stars moon at night.
Days flowed soft
And time seemed silent
All seemed most
Like I wanted it
To be.
I had just a
Splendoriously- wonderful
Time camping I did,
I did- yes- I did.

Start

Try to start
By finishing
The old on the
Old day
Then start
The new day
As new,
Its better
Works better,
That way.

159

Hawk

A hawk picked up
A small puppy
To eat one day carried it to,
About 30 feet high
The puppy from
The hawk fell away
A small boy the puppy
Did find
And took the puppy
For a friend and
To be kind.
The hawk all this
Did see in a tree
Close but away,
And flew away
Hungry but happy
Maybe not happy
That day
Cause… its meal slipped away.

Bugs

A bug, a bug, do you
Like bugs
Do you like plastic
Bugs?
They cannot crawl
They cannot move
They do just what
You make them do
They look like bugs
And if you like bugs
Hey
If you do
A plastic bug can be
That bug– a bug
A real nice bug
The bug the bug
For you.

Tired

I must have
Been tired today
I sat down
In a chair
In a room by myself
With no one
In the house but myself
no one...
In the house, but myself
About 1:30 till 4:00 AM
In the chair
I really must
Have been tired
Or felt that way
When I sat down
In the chair
That day.

Met

We met on a crowded Okinawan bus on the island
Of Okinawa
Coming home from a day
Of work performing
Military duty
Mr. Holland in the Air force
Myself in the army.
We met on the crowded
Very crowded bus– with
Standing room only
Which permitted us to speak
To each other.
And find out our homes
Were quite near each other
That our wives were Japanese
We became good friends
This friendship has remained
Thru the years.
From our meeting on the crowded
Okinawan bus– on Okinawa of
Far, far away– that seems
As only… yesterday.

What Be It

Happy happy
What be it be?
Not the same to you, to me
Not the same to me to you
Happy, happy
Be it, it be….
What we've seen
And
What we see
Of-
What we think
That makes…
Happy to us,
Be.

Joy-Happiness

Inside joy, from
Deep within
Is of the
Creators-creation
Happiness is
Unpredictable-
Temporary, and
Comes from another
Story.
While inside joy from
Deep within
Is of the
Creators, creation.

Seems

Over the years it seems
It's the small things
You remember
Like the bells ringing
On the cow's neck
When she shook her head
Out in the country where cows roamed
And rang the bell.
Or like the bell in the
Old country school
On the roof– the teacher rang
By pulling a rope
To end recess time.
Also the whistle of
A steam passenger or freight
Train in the country
Going by
The whip poor wills call
Or swooping call, of night hawks
At night
Over the years it seems
It's the small things you remember.
And…
The choices of family
Old friends
Old places
Too
You remember
They're still there
Though changed
So have you
Since you, went
Thru.
Over the years
Its seems… it seems.

A Light

Sometime we shine
In some thing's
In others the light
Seems to us
Not quite as much.
But– its there,
Keep the light
Just shining
To guide others
Thru dark– a light
Of bright
To see to guide
To touch.

Dreams

Independent all along
To make it to a place
You won
You never had before
Is a dream to have
If one can dream
A dream worth striving for
For then one can be
More independent all alone
To think with others
And with others
Helping helping
Working together
Independent all alone
Can independently
Miraculously achieve
The fact that dreams
Those dreams, you dream
Sometime they do
Come thru– to true
For you.

The Rainbow

I've heard that
Clouds drift over the rainbow
but rainbows are so
High in the sky
Yet,
Clouds drift by
Like sunshine high.
Clouds come after the storm
Rainbows too-they come after a storm
And are beautiful too
To let us know– the storm has passed
Its thru, its thru
The storm that storm passed thru
Clouds could at that time
Drift
I guess clouds could drift…
Over the rainbow
I heard they do I wonder if butterflies do?
I've heard that…
Clouds drift over the rainbow
Have you heard that too?

A Record

A note is a record
Of time gone by
That shows how time
And moments
Doth fly
Also showing
How notes can in a way keep as record
In a slight
Teenk see weenk see
Bit
Or slight sliver
Of that second
Slight moment
Of wonderful
Kindly beautiful
Time
That imagery…
These notes.

Train

I hear the whistle
Can't you too
The trains a comin
For some one too
Conductors gotten
His step stool down
Trains a comin for someone
Trains a comin to town
The railroads long gone
Years ago
That's ok whistles blowin
For someone hear it blow.
Trains a comin
Don't need a ticket
Or any rails
Just get on board, you ain't a comin back
Cause you just be a ridin ridin
Ridin to somewhere
Ridin on those, magic rails.

Thru Clouds

Just why on
Cloudy days
The sun does not
Appear to shine
But really does shine
On high in the sky unseen
For clouds they
Cover the sky
To understand sometime
Is difficult at times
We wonder why
Sometime perhaps
The things we want
And think they are what
We really need
Right then
Are not for us
Is hard to understand
But comes when needed
By a higher helping hand
With understanding
Much later and why…like sunshine as light
Thru clouds
On high.

Soon

I just seen
Two big crows
Fly out of that tree and
Just where they
Were going?
I really don't know
They didn't tell me.
Those two
Big crows I,
Just seen.

Night Quiet

Quiet of the night
To the lonely
Is as dark of night
Like light of day
Noisy
Also thunderous
No-
Is more as dawn
When sun awakens
Day,
From dark…
Nights quiet
It's way

Ghost Dog

On the isle of wight
Off the England coast
I'm told
There be the ghost
Of a dog
Of black I'm told
With feet of white
That may come to
Save you if quick tide
Comes quiet and in the water
Catches you.
I'm told
This dog of ghost
Or ghost of dog
Seems to walk on
The water and disappears
Too after it
Saves you
I'm told of this
That it exists
On the isle of Wight
Off the coast of England.
If you sometime
go there
You…
Might check on it
Too.
And…
Thank you

Your Heart

Your heart can tell you
What to do where to go
So listen good
Listen close
Before you leave before
You go
Your heart speaks slow
Your heart speaks low
Your heart listen to it. Listen to it
Listen close
Listen good
Listen, listen
For it speaks slow, low
Its good– it loves you
And can tell you
What to do where to go
Many good things
You should know
If you just…
Listen to it– your heart,
Listen. Listen.

Flying

One crow
On the housetop
That crow
Flew away– it's ok
Crows are flying
Somewhere
Everyday.

164

Before

Right before you left it came
I didn't understand what it was
Something over came me
I think you understood what it was
But said nothing
You didn't want to upset me
With your call to leave
We had been together
For so long– but I think
You know as the faint notes
Of a song the tune
Of faint music your call
From far your song a tuned
For you I think you knew
As you watched as you listened
Still it effects me and
Always will
I now understand more and
Appreciate in a way different
The days the years the weeks
As they pour as they flow as rivers snake, meander
Life's way daily with each
Differently very differently
Of the me that I see that I feel
As I see the me in the mirror
Life's mirror that…
Right before you left perhaps
Days weeks you understood
You knew and silently
I would finally understand more
As life itself pours
With silence thru
And I am and I appreciate
All and lovely
For love knows.

Pictures in the Sky

In a sky of blue
The clouds that drift by
They paint pictures in this way
For all to see
High very high , way up
In the sky
Oh just look at that
Horse over there
See look, look
Right over there
And that cow
That sheep
An alligator too
Look, look that elephant
On the tricycle
He's an odd fellow passing thru
Can't you see them?
Yes I do
In a sky of blue
The clouds that drift by
Paint pictures in the sky.

Rolling

The rolling of the ocean
as morning fog
just slithers away
brings in the morning hours
in kind of
just
extra special
beautiful
pristine-ways.

165

Surfers

Surfers on the ocean
ride ocean waves
for free
and the ocean
tosses them
back to shore
care free
cheer fully.

Everyday

A life must be
Encouraged
Right at start to life's
End with being honest praised
Of being kind
To send
A life with
Respect
Of all to
Right thru
To life's end
A life must be encouraged
With some, best
All of these
Thoughts some way…
Everyday.

The Call

He answered the call quietly left
In his own special way
And the call comes to all
Waits to hear
Of their way
While the mountains are still
While the wind rustles still
The birds, all love… waits
For answered call
Seconds, days, months, years-
Pass tho small wait
For the call from love
Is with absence of time
And grows as life
Smooth rough sublime
Calling silent so silent all the time.
We all follow the call day by day
Tho different pathes may lead us astray
Only thru love actions memories
Will we or others know
The depth of our heart
Forgiveness too
That shelters the call
That accompanies us thru
And is answered our own
Special way
Tho love understands all
Spiritually
Silently lovely, and– it's
Forever– when we're called
To leave into forever.

The World

Why does corn
Make so much silk
Just to grow?
I don't know
Why do birds and butterflies
Fly so quiet in the sky?
I don't know
Why is up so high
And down so low?
I don't know, I don't know
But this I know
I do I do
That true love
Is true, is true
That singing songs
And laughing too
Is good for you
Is good for you
I know of this for
I've done this too I know
That true love is true
And having singings
Good for you
Just why about corn
The silk of corn
Why birds and butterflies
Fly quiet
Why up is high
And down so low
don't worry. don't worry
All that is ok
The world has and
Accepts it all the way
go have yourself
A beautiful day
And rest at night
That way
And…
Bye.

Golden Day

After someone a loved one slips away
Discreetly silently
In a house, the house
Seems to accept and
Speaks silently in its own
Home way
You accept and understand
Or, you become the
Home– that houses silent, a
Foe that silently with the
One the house
Remembers the houses own way
Perhaps forever of you
Its seems
One must accept in orderly ways
True love as love comes
Day by golden day.
After a loved one slips away.

Happens

It happens to you
It happens to me
It happens to everybody
By golly by ghee
You look in the mirror
And say and see
And see and say
Hey…
Im getting older
Is that really me?
It happens to you
It happens to me
It happens to everybody
By golly by ghee.

Quiet

Quiet in this house– so quiet,
Not even a mouse
Cats in the garage
Asleep quiet there too
Goes outside sometime
Garage quiet too
So quiet this house
Guess quiets, quiet
That's why
Its quiet.

Re-told

As the days go by
There's a tendency
To remember
The days of old
And how they
Could be seemingly should be
Somehow
Told re-told
But that would be surprisingly unpopular
Except to others
Who think
Perhaps
As you or just
Pretend too.
Still its ok
When one should choose
And remember
And perhaps write down
On paper what and
How one remembers
The days of old
Your days of old
And how to you
They should be
Remembered
By yourself by you…
To you... retold.
As, the days-
Go by.

Tints

The shade of evening
Tints the sky
Soon
The hours of dark
Of night
The stars, the moon
Will own the sky
The shade of evening
Tints the sky.

Calling

Say… listen to me, I'm talking to you
I hear the birds
I hear the birds
I hear the birds calling
Listen, listen
Oh… listen
The haunting, call
Of the pigeon birds
I heard the birds
I heard the birds
Did you hear the birds?
Did you
Hear the birds?
The birds…
The birds– they
Were calling, they
Were calling, calling
Calling, calling
Calling
The birds
Were calling
Did you hear the birds? I heard the birds
I heard the birds
I heard the birds.
The haunting call...of-
The pigeon, birds.

Been Thru

When ones been thru
The rough the tough
Storms are no problem
The helmsman
Steers guides one
Right thru
With ease, smiles
Most all the way
Life's a breeze…
When ones been thru
The rough the tough.

Something

Write me something
For Christmas
Say its still July
Well write me something
For July
That started with June
And that full
Round moon
Of June with its
Abundance of room
Yes…
Write me something
Of
Christmas with the
Full of the moon
The warmth of July
And where the sunlight
Of love doth lie
Oh yes…
Write me something
Something for
Christmas
The Christmas of June
The moon and
July.

Gracefully

I'm watching
The limbs and green leaves
On yonder tall tree
Flow gracefully to and fro, to and fro
With the breeze
Against white clouds
In the sky
Flowing just flowing
To and fro, to and fro
As graceful, graceful dances
Dancing, dancing
Gracefully oh so very
Gracefully
With the wind
The breezes
The white clouds of evening
And the sky
I'm watching its beautiful
Just beautiful.

Be Careful

The mountain lions, the mountain lions
Be careful of the mountain lions
I'm told…
They're here, they're here
They're everywhere
I've looked, I've looked
For the mountain lions
I've looked most everywhere,
And I haven't seen one anywhere
Perhaps they've seen me
From great distance
And of me they have
Great fear
Boo-oo-oo-oo to you
Mountain lion
For you too
I have great fear
The mountain lion, the mountain lion
Be careful of the
Mountain lions.

Flying Moths

The scrub oak area
I am camping in
Near a valley far below
Has several oak tree
Flying moths
That are flying this
Time of season
Seemingly every where
Every where on this
Bright blue windy day
Aloft
Gracefully happily here
Today
Helping to make interesting..
The day.

Painted

I've been watching
A large black spider
On a tree
Appearing to climb
A scrub oak
Tree
But not moving
Then checked
Why it never
Moves
Someone painted it
On the tree
The spider I've
Been watching
Can never get
Up the tree
Because
It's painted
In a spot
That hardly moves
on a
Living scrub
Oak tree.

Clouds Drift

A few clouds of white with more then more
I see now
Drifting slowly before twilight
In the sky—the blue of sky
I guess to cover the sky
Before
The night of darkness
covers the sky
When dark
Completely
covers the sky
There's
The dark
And you…
And of course
I
Tho know
A few clouds of white
With more then more
Drifting quietly-make hazy,
Before twilight– evening
In the sky, the blue
Of sky.

Folks

It's hard to meet someone
Not too tall
Not too short
Not too skinny
Not too fat
Not too mean
not too happy
Most folks all folks
Come as they are
I'm like that
Maybe you are too
Most folks are
If they're true
It's hard to meet someone
Other ways
On most days.

Family Gathering

With a view of the ocean
Thru large windows too
Where boats bobbed floated
On waves of the ocean
And distant shores
There to see
Our family dined
To a fantastic dinner
At the Saporro restaurant
In Monterey, CA
A celebration
And a happy birthday
Dinner for Michael my grandson
Which was just a
Wonderful beautiful family gathering
On
This day of
July 21, 2012.

Given

Talents given
To each very different
Determine our
Places and travel
Thru life
The places we go
Have went been
Are much determined
By our talents
The trying or
Greatly achieving
Of our talents…
Given.

Something

Write me something
For Christmas
Say its still July
Well write me
Something
For July
That started
With June
And that full
Round moon
Of June with its
Abundance of room
Yes…
Write me something
Of
Christmas with the
Full of moon
The warmth of July
And where the sunlight
Of love
Doth lie
Oh yes…
Write me something
Something for
Christmas
The Christmas of June the moon and July

Disappeared

A child I did know
From years years ago
Just where did it go?
When it disappeared
Into an adult
Years years ago.

Existed

Please
Do not disturb the
Moment
For this has restored
The dream
The dream that is of
What was that passed
In the golden of times
When the rainbows of now
Was in infancy
And the now practically covers the all
Please
Do not disturb the moment
For we did not
Realize it even
Existed....
At all.

Play

Cold, hot
Rainy, windy, icy
Cloudy, sunny, snowy
All that's
Ok too
As long as
We play
Outside
That's really...
What I want
To do.

Choo-Choo

Look at that old
Choo-choo train
Its bell just rings
A ding a ling ling
It puffs it smokes
And everything
Its fun to watch
That old
Choo- choo train.

Just to

Oh just to
Run and jump
Yell, smell
Dig, build
Imagine too
Now...
That's what I want
To do.

One

One can make a big
Difference
Good or bad
Tho only one maybe
Think of one healthy
Mosquito and you
With that mosquito
To be one entire
Night
One tiny mosquito
Makes a big difference
In a night
One only one can…
Make a difference.

Ceased

What used to be
Has not ceased to be
don't look for it
Its just
Not there anymore
All tends to move on
Even you.
It's at times difficult
To admit
But admit it
We must and…
With most deep
Deepest of trust
Progress is and
Always will be
For the growth
Of humanity.
What used to be must…
Cease to be
Its gone
Disappeared
From the race
Replaced with new and…
Its about time
Its about time.

Painting

Painting of feet from paint on feet
Paining of hands form paint on hands
Made by feet
And hands
By children on paper
Are special in a way
Will keep for days
Weeks years
As hands and feet grow
Their way
And also all can see
Small hands and feet
That stay
The same as the feet and hands
That painted them on
That special day on paper
The paints of
Those little feet
And hands.

Blends

Just being alone
After having lost
One you've been with
For nearly 60 years
Is like being the only
Stone left
In a large yard
visible like the sun
In the sky
All know the sun
Is the sun
And must always be
Tho one
The same for the stone
All have known
For years
Nearly 60 thru
As family

continued

continues ...Blends

For family most
Still they be
The family of 2
They regard you as
One to be
Tho they know you
Of one to be
Most know not what
To do
So nothing most do
And lonely grows
When alone with you, as
This one lives - silent inside deep
This one being the only
After years together
As two now, must learn
To do
Tho sharing with
Others
One finds
Alone and stone
Plus lovely
The same much
In a way
And surrounded
By lovely
Still the feeling
Of the only stone
Left in a yard
Or
The only sun
In the sky
Visible
Drifts by
And
Love lovely
Blends blends
Plus
Plus feelings
Thru.

The There-the Hear

I hear voices
And there's no one there
I talk to you
And you don't hear
You talk to me
We look we see
I think you think
Folks aren't there
You are here
I am here
Something's wrong
What is wrong?
The there the here
The song I hear oh that music
The strange to me
No one can see the what I see
Nor can they hear
They think I imagine
But I hear, I feel
this strange to me
I hear…
And there– you are.

Early Years

After the early years of marriage
And small things
Are talked and smooth
Worked out
Then the two
Can consider most
Settling
Together is
Done
The two can then become as one
After the early years
Are done.

Love

The morning sun
As it lights the sky
Form morning till noon
To the travelers eye
Is clear if clouds
Are not in view
And even then
The travelers eye view
From noon till night
Thru twilight evening
Night till dawn
And morning again
Is not obscured even tho…
Clouds and storms may come
For the traveler
Has traveled
With a faith eternal
That guides to
Creation golden
Morning sunrise
Given thru
Faith hope memories
And eternal
Love.

A Hunter

I never was a hunter
Of wild animals
No not I
I marvel at wild
Animals at least
Most kinds I try
The snakes I do not
Get around in
Their space
I let them be
But others to see
Most others
I marvel when
Them I see
And feel good
That we can
Share this world
Where that
We be
I never was a hunter
Of wild animals
No not I
I marvel at wild animals
At least most kinds I try.

The Body

All parts of the body
Are happy with each
And are happy
To share
Anything the body
Can teach
For all parts
Of the body
Are happy to be
All things
That the body
As one– complete,
In body
Can be.

Labors

All the labors
Along lifes road
One carries thru
Must be
Carefully
Balanced and carried
As one passes thru
On the shoulders
Of the one
With creation
Carrying…
The labors,
thru.

175

Kinda

If you want to
Think about things
And be kinda healthy medically
Remember as long
As you can
Eat sleep
And…
go to the restroom
Why you could maybe
Hop on a rocket
And go to the moon
But if you cannot
Do either one of those
Three
Why old friendly friend
You're no longer
Kinda healthy
Medically
As you oughta
Be
Right about then.

Put

Put things away put things away
Put things away
Do I have to?
Yes
Put things away
Put things away
Put things away
Gosh do I have to?
Yes..
But its fun to be messy
I know I like to be messy to
But put things away
Put things away
Ohhhh k.

Something's

Some things maybe
We come across
In life are kinda
Best left alone
And like they are
To be
And if you stir
Em up they get
They become
A really fright
To see
Some things maybe
In life
Survive
That way
Designed that way
Think others
Are strange
That way
Contribute to life
That way
And as long as they
don't bother anything
That way
May be…
Some things
We come across in life are kinda
Best left alone
And like they are
To be.

Unfolds

Life unfolds
That way
We sort of
Read It like a book
As we travel our way
And see others
Traveling where
We've traveled
Traveling their way
We can assist
If we can
But must be careful
Of soggy land
So as not to upset
The entire of
Life's plan
Then step lightly along
Life's plan
For life unfolds
That way
We can sort of
Read it like a book
As we travel
Our way

Of Day

Its daytime now
I can see the light of dawn
Daytime is coming
On
The night has drifted away
Where has it gone
Time seems like
It was only
Yesterday
My goodness
Its bedtime now
What happened to the day
Its bedtime now
I can see the light of day

Of This

Sometime
You think of this
As years pass
And they do
You think of this
When your spouse of
Years nearly 60
Has left called away
A few years past
You're alone only one
In your home
You think of others
In years past
That have done the same
When they were left
Their spouse called
Called to leave sometime
They too crossed
This bridge in life
That you now do
At that time you thought not
Of it as you
Now do
But life has now
Changed.
Changed for you
And your time
in life has come
As you cross over
That bridge
That bridge in life
As one passing thru
Sometime
You think of this
As years pass
And they do pass.

Blossoms of Spring

The season the season
The season of spring
It seems that most all things
Appear to start as
A season of spring
When the snows the cold
Of winter is over
And all is a blossom
With flowers of spring
The blossoms are then to flower
And then to grow, grow, grow
Produce seeds that do same
Then this cycle continues
As years then be
Into eternities
This is where real life
Enters in
For most of this cycling
Goes as planned.
Beautifully wonderfully
Meeting all demands
And cycles, cycles years
Years, years lovely thru
Others in the season of spring
They stay
Hardly ever seem to get
Away
From blossoms to flower
their seeds know not
In fact they seem to kind of rot
From spring to summer
But then they're thru
Tho some get beautiful all
The way to winter as planned
Cycling by cycles from spring
On thru from
The season of spring
The season of spring
It seems all things start
To blossom somewhat
as the blossoms of spring
the blossoms of spring.

For Everybody

No one ever
Thinks they're
Gonna get old
But they do
There's enough old
In aging
Stored
For everybody
You and me too
If they ever do
Get low on old
Why…
The sun and the moon
And the years
And the months
And the days
Hours, minutes
Seconds too
Always.
Carry surplus
Of old
With them
To quickly fill
Any supply low
Supply
Of old quickly
Like a soft
Summer breeze passes thru.
There's always enough
Old for everyone
You and me too
As we pass thru
Tho,
No one even
Thinks that they're
Gonna get old
But we do.

Came

The summer came
And June, July was here
Then August too
And September
Summer finished
Autumn was here
Summer was beautiful
Autumn too
With summers green
Leaves grass
Autumns lovely of colors
Tho soon finished
Thru
Most lovely of seasons
Passed mysteriously thru
With rapidity
And now in snows of winter
I remember
The seasons of
Summer autumn
In warmth and love.

Ok

When you're all alone
And no ones in the house
For years but only you
Sometime you make
Odd noise
Talk to only you at times
Then wonder why
Maybe or
Perhaps
Its because it's the me in you
That wants to entertain
The you in you
Maybe that's the reasons why
When you're all alone
And no ones there but you
You sometime talk to you
Until
You're thru
Or answer you.

Spotted

I went camping and folks
Talked about the mountain lions
Mountain lions
Mountain lions folks
Talked about the mountain lions
I seen no mountain lion
There but I looked
I looked, I looked carefully
That I did
And spotted a little lizard
Who spotted me there
We exchanged glances
The lizard hesitated just a bit
And then it was off and away
Twas the last I seen of it
I seen no mountain lions
But seen a lizard tho
When I went camping the
Other day

Beans

Breakfast dinner supper too
What will you have
Hey you, hey you
I'll have bean soup
Cornbread
That's what I'll do
Sorry only beans for you
Cornbread went
With the morning crew
Breakfast dinner supper too
Beans is all there is for you
Hey you, hey you
Beans is all there is for you.
So, have some beans
Hey– you.

Talking Singing

Talking talking
don't talk at me
Talk to me
Singing, singing
don't sing at me
Sing to me
Make me guess
Make me guess
And imagine
What your smooth
Of voice might
Bring forth next and be
To me to me
don't sing at me
don't sing at me
Sing, sing, sing to me
With me
And sing to me

Writing

Writing poetry gives me a way
To see and in a way
Kind of feel and see
The things I think and see
And feel
In a way kind of and
A way others
Kind of do not
Kind of feel and think and see them
Their way quickly
Writing poetry my way
Does that for me
In its way and helps me silently
Pass the hours they seem to drift as I write
Soft quiet slow
Away
Day or night their way.

Drift

I can hear the clock
Its telling me soft
By ticking away
Ever so soft that
You've wasted the day
For your timing was off
You stayed up too late
The day of today
Has passed by
The hour now is of late
Night with dark is near
The clock
The clock I can hear the clock
Telling me even soft that
You've wasted the day
Your timing is off
You stayed up too late
The day of today
Has passed nearly by
Night is near
And I the clock know not
Of day of night know not
You of days of nights know
Watch them come watch them go
Your style your way
I the clock tell only of the
Seconds, minutes, hours, you use your way
As you let them drift, drift, drift away.

At a Time

One rung at a time
That is the way that
The ladder must be
Climbed one rung just one rung
One rung at a time
Two is too much
It tires one to much
Climb the ladder
Life's ladder too
Just…
One rung one rung
Only one rung at
At a time.

Of Evening

In the evening
That's when the birds
Start to get quiet
For soon most sleep
In the evening
That's when the sun
Gets low in the sky
And seems close
But not close by
In the evening
That's when the hills
Around seem real quiet
They're there but
Not a sound in the evening
That's when twilights
Saying goodbye to day
Its near time to
Slip away for
Twilights time of day
In the evening
That's when everything
Takes on a slight
But darkness glow
And then in a blue dark
Sky appears a star, that-
Peeps thru and soon
Very soon more
And then the moon with
Stars make soft
Mysterious light with
Sounds mid secrets
Of the night
Also darkness tiptoes in
The evening
That's when daylight
Twilight evening
Rests
For night the
Free soft dark of night appears
In the evening in the evening
In the evening.

Each Day

To behold the dawn each morning
To behold the noontime
Too and the twilight then
The evening
The evening is a blessing
Surely
It is too
Also the night
When it arrives with stars
With moon
Moonlight
Milky way
Oh the ways the many ways
These blessing are lovely to behold
With love in love
Each day
Is just wondrous.

Songs

Crucifixion

Arranged by Gianni Staiano

AL VICENT

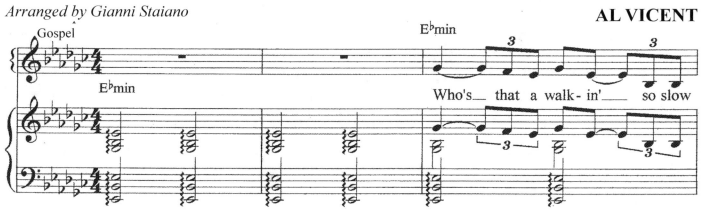

Who's__ that a walk-in'____ so slow

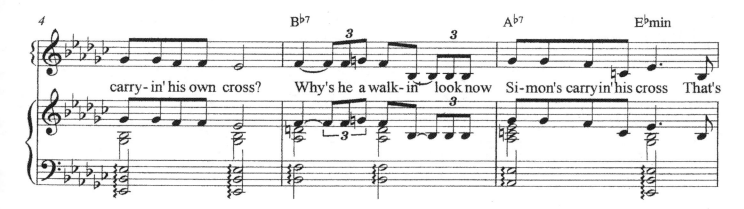

carry-in' his own cross? Why's he a walk-in' look now Si-mon's carryin' his cross That's

Je - sus a carry in' the sins of the world That's Je - sus a carry in' the

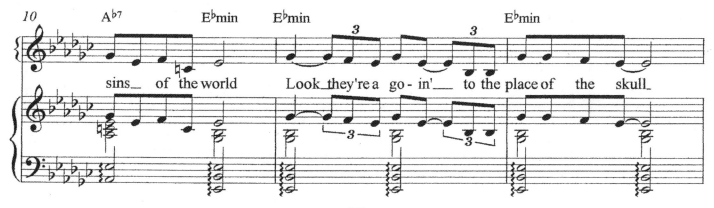

sins__ of the world Look they're a go - in'___ to the place of the skull__

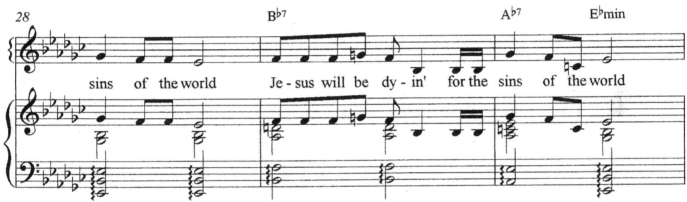

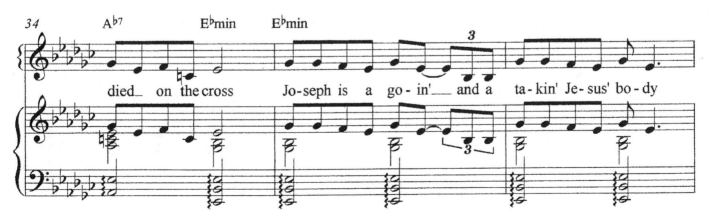

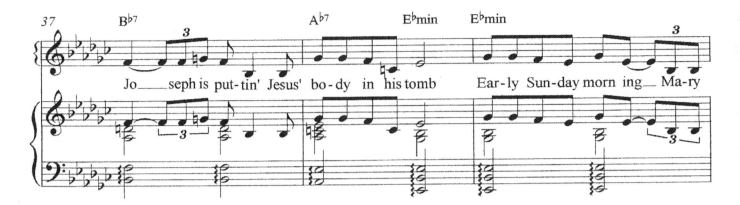

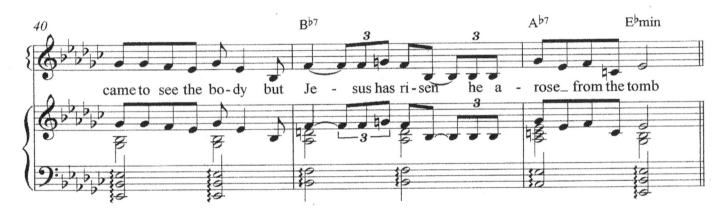

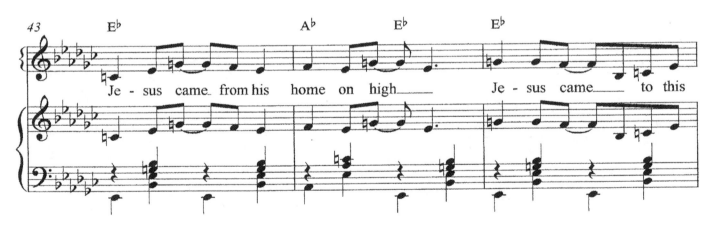

he'll re - turn____ oh he'll come back a - gain____

Stories

The Enchabted Rug

Jody Curtis and her little brother Germaine were always together. They had a lot of other friends but they always seemed to be together and not far from each other. Jody was eight years old and Germaine was only six. Jody could run really really fast, faster than any of the boys in her school and in her grade. She was in the fourth grade and head of her class too. Now Germaine, he liked to explore and try to understand how everything was and how it seemed to be. Even rolly polly insects, he would pick them up and touch them, then watch them roll up and eventually unroll and crawl away. He always let them go. He would even studied snails and watch them crawl, bird and rabbits too.

All his friends would watch him. Sometimes they would pick up insects and watch birds with Germaine, but not for long. They would leave and soon do something else. Jody likes to read and Germaine did too. Together they always would be found in the library at school and usually always at home after homework was finished. Their parents thought this was great because libraries have good information for children and everyone. Jody and Germaine loved to go there and just look at books and all the information they could find, especially lots of pictures about places they could travel and see. Things like insects, birds, animals, and all kinds of castles, sailing ships, whales, large octopus, dolphins, almost anything they thought was important to them. Jody and Germaine wanted and were hungry for this kind of information.

They just loved to go to their grandparents place. Their grandparents lived in a small town with a pretty big farm in an old old house. It was a big house with lots of rooms and one room they liked more than any of the other rooms of course. They liked all the rooms but this one was the very very best because it was on the side of the house where you could see the trees. They can see the open sky and in the evening they can see the moon come up, rising over a big big mountain that seemed close but was really far away.

At night it was quiet, so quiet that when it was dark you could hear insects like crickets and also frogs and animals speaking to their friends. Their grandparents place was out of town by itself, which seemed to Jody and Germaine like a little place. A little enchanted place where they loved to go spend time with their grandparents where it was quiet, where they could run and play and have lots of fun.

Grandma and Grandpa lived in a small town in Idaho which was a long way from where Jody and Germaine lived. That was ok because their parents had told them they were going on vacation and could stay for three weeks. Their mother and father were also going, but could only stay for one week and Jody and Germaine could stay with Grandma and Grandpa for an additional two weeks. School was out for the summer and they could just have a nice time. Jody was so happy she told Germaine, "Isn't this just great we can be with Grandma Ruth and Grandpa Joseph for three weeks."

"Yes" said Germaine, "I'm really happy. I really like to visit with Grandma and Grandpa. It's really nice there. I can see lots of things on Grandma and Grandpa's farm."

About a week later, everything was ready. Father, mother, Jody and Germaine all went to the airport, boarded an airplane and flew to their grandparent's farm in far away Idaho. For Jody and Germaine it was a wonderful trip because it was their very first airplane ride. They were excited. They talked about the airplane, read about airplanes and gathered all the information they could find on how it would feel to actually really fly in the air like birds do all the time.

It was nothing new for their mother and father, they had been on airplanes many times, but for Jody and her brother Germaine this was different. They found it very new and scary but very nice too. When they got on the airplane and went to their seats, they saw that it was a large airplane. The seats were in a long row and many people sat in their row. They sat next to their mother and father. Father sat on the outside next to the isle. It was exciting. When all the people were seated and the airplane started to move, Jody asked her father, "What's happening? What are we going to do?"

Father told Jody, "You and Germaine just listen to the attendant talking. She is telling everybody what to do. Soon we will be in the air. Fasten your seat belt, make sure your seat back is all the way up and all your bags are stored under your seat so nothing will fall and hurt anyone because soon we will be flying."

"Like birds?" Jody said. "Like birds?" Germaine was listening too.
Germaine said, "Wow Jody, just like we read about in the library book. We'll be flying soon! Dad just said so. Mom, mom, dad said we'll be in the air soon! I'm happy, I'm really happy; I want to fly like birds. I like birds."

Father said again, "Now everyone check and make sure your seat belt is tight, your seat back is up all the way."
The airplane attendant was finished talking and was walking up and down the aisle checking everyone.
Mother said "Germaine just sit and wait now, soon we will be in the air on our way to grandma and grandpa's place." Jody and Germaine were very excited. Jody reached over and punched Germaine.
Germaine hollered "Stop Jody! Stop hitting I didn't do anything."

"I know you didn't Germaine, I'm excited Germaine, we'll be in the air soon like dad said, I want you to know."
"I know Jody, I heard dad talking too."
"Okay, I'm sorry," said Jody.
Father spoke up and said "Jody, Germaine, stop fighting and sit still, watch and listen to what the airplane does."
The airplane had moved to the long runway where it has to go real fast to go in the air and fly. Dad said, "Listen, be quiet and watch. The pilot must get the okay to move." "Okay dad," said Jody and Germaine "we'll listen." And they did.

Soon they heard and felt the airplane engine start going fast the airplane started to move. It started moving faster, and faster, and faster. They saw it passing everything on the ground fast, real fast. Soon Jody and Germaine felt the whole airplane lift off the ground as they looked out the window.
"Jody, Jody!" Germaine hollered, "Jody we're flying, we're flying, we're in the air like birds and we're flying. Just like the book in the library said, we're flying!"
"I know, I know" said Jody, "I see it too." "I just wanted you to know." Then Germaine punched Jody. "Jody, now we're even."
Mom said, "Germaine, Jody, you two stop."

The airplane kept going up, up, up, climbing then it leveled off, they could see that the sky was nice and blue. The clouds were puffy white way down below them. The airplane was high in the sky. Jody and Germaine said, "Wow, this is nice."

At lunch time, the attendant served everyone a nice lunch, and after lunch the airplane landed at a large airport. Father and mother picked up the bags, rented a car, and after driving a few hours, they were at grandma and grandpa's place. Grandma and grandpa had been waiting and were happy to see everybody.

After lots of hugs and kisses, explaining all the details about their trip, and putting their bags in their rooms, grandma and grandpa started to tell about the rug they had recently put in the house and about the people who installed the rug.

Grandpa said, "One day maybe about two years ago your grandmother and I were sitting on the porch, it was a nice afternoon. Grandma said it would be nice if we put a new rug in the house because our old rug is getting worn and old." Grandpa said they talked about what color the rug should be and what kind of rug they wanted. They also talked about install rug in some of the rooms that do not have it now, especially the room that Jody and Germaine like so much.

Grandpa said, "We thought maybe a real nice, tough, soft, deep feeling rug would be nice for that room. We did not know where we could find a rug like that, but we talked about it anyway then we kind of forgot about the rug as the afternoon progressed. But later grandma talked a little bit more about the rug then I think we went to the little room you folks like and talked about the special rug we wanted for that room."

Grandma said, "Yes, we did, it seemed like just a lot of different ideas and thoughts came about a rug for that room much more than the rug for the rest of the house. We thought the rug for that room should be extra soft to lie on, even if it gets dirty it can almost clean itself. It will always feel soft and warm even if it's very cold outside and that at night it could be kind of special to help you find your bed at night. We kind of talked about things we thought children would think of if choosing a rug for a room they liked. In the room that night grandma said, "We had a good time, we felt like children again. It was great, we had fun." Then we talked about rugs, the type we wanted for the other rooms and walked all through the house talking about the rugs."

Jody's mother said, "Why did you think so much about the rug, you could have just gone to town, picked out a rug, and had the company come out and put it in."

Jody's father said, "Yes, why didn't you do that?"

Grandpa said, "Yes, that's what we were going to do and grandma talked about the rug some more that evening because we hadn't thought much about the rug before since it had been there many years and this is an old house."

Then grandma said, "Let us finish the story and tell you what happened that evening while we were discussing the rug together, grandpa and I. Germaine, we were about to step out of the room you and Jody like and we looked down and two rather large rolly polly bugs, larger than we have ever seen, seemed like they were looking at us and wanted to crawled right past us right into the room. But they didn't and it was strange the way they acted, like maybe they going to do something. I never seen rolly polly's act like that before. Then two rather large crickets looked at us and walked right past us over to the two rolly polly's and it looked like they discussed something together."

"We were watching. This is very strange," grandma said. "This is strange. What are they doing? I have never seen rolly polly's and crickets talk like that together."

"Me either" grandpa said. "But let's watch what happens next."

"Then we saw one rolly polly start crawling very fast one way around the room and the other rolly polly crawled the other way around the room and they met in the middle," grandpa said. "Looks like they are measuring this room."

"Yes I'm watching. This certainly is strange," grandma said.

The crickets watched the rolly polly's while they were working, then the crickets walked to different corners of the room and then started walking to cross as an x in the middle of the room. When they finished the rolly polly's and the crickets met together as if they were discussing something, then the crickets started to sing. First one then the other cricket began singing. They sang for maybe three or four times and they sang beautifully. Together they sounded almost like our song Twinkle twinkle little star.

Grandpa said, "Something that can hardly be believed happened next. The rolly polly's and the crickets waited together after the crickets finished singing. One of the windows in the little room was about half open. We heard something like a bumble bee flying but the sound was loud like a very large bumble bee. In flew a large black bumble bee with white wings that was about three times as large as a regular bumble bee. It looked at us, flew right over to where the rolly polly's and crickets were and landed. It then walked over to the crickets and rolly polly's and it looked like they were discussing something for a few seconds. Then the bumble bee flew through all the rooms and circled around in each room. We had talked about rendering the old rugs and rooms."

Grandpa continued his story and said, "The crickets and rolly polly's waited while the bumble bee was flying around in the rooms. When the bumble bee finished, the bee landed again where the rolly pollys and the crickets were, stayed a few seconds, flew to the open window where it originally came in through. Then the bee turned and went to the other window in the room."

"Jody, you and Germaine like to listen to frogs, crickets, insects, and animals that watch the moon come over that big mountain. All that is magical but I must tell you, the other window in the room was closed and when the bee came near it, it opened like magic."

"We watched, we didn't believe our eyes. This could not be happening but it was. We both saw all of it. The rolly pollys coming in and then the crickets coming in. The rolly polly's were crawling around like they were measuring the room. The crickets doing the same thing and the large bee coming in discussing something with the rolly pollys and the crickets. Then flying through all the rooms that we wanted to install rugs and finally flying to the window that opened as if by magic when it flew out.

"All this is strange, very strange, so let me tell you what happen next," said grandma.

"Grandpa and I looked at each other; we had never seen anything like this happen before. Our eyes just opened wide and we opened our mouth as we looked at each other. Then we turned around to see where the rolly pollys and crickets were and they were gone. Whether they went out to the window or just where, we will never know. But they were not anywhere we could see in the room. Also when we turned back to look at the window where the bee flew out of, it was closed like it had never been opened. The other window it came into, that was half open was still opened like we left it.

Jody said, "Wow grandpa, grandma that sounds like something we read about in the library books."

"Maybe this rug is an enchanted rug or something," Germaine said.

"Yes it could or might be," said Jody.

Jody and Germaine's father and mother said, "Why didn't you tell us this before?"

"We would have told you," said grandma and grandpa, "but you probably wouldn't have believed us and said we were just getting old, imagining these things. But these things all happened." Now like Jody and Germaine said, it could be an enchanted rug since so many strange things have happened concerning this rug around this farm."

"We don't say much about it to others; maybe no one would believe us," said grandpa.

"It really could be an enchanted rug as we said. We had no thought about that you know. The people that later installed the rug, they were also very strange. After they finished installing the rugs in our house, they insisted on leaving a rug, a large piece of rug too. They said to keep the piece of rug here and it was for Jody and Germaine, your grandchildren. We never used the rug; right now it's in the closet over there. It's in the closet sometimes, but sometimes we find it all over. Sometimes we hear a noise in this room. We look and the rug is gone, it might be in another room for awhile, then it comes back here again."

"Yes it might be enchanted," said grandma.

"Jody you and Germaine check it out. The people that put the rug down said it was for you two. Now the people that installed that rug, let me tell you" said grandpa. "It's quite a story too. One morning grandma and I were sitting at the table. I had just finished eating some hot cakes crispy fried bacon and eggs. A nice breakfast, grandma was drinking coffee. We looked out the window and there was this huge, I mean really huge white horse standing. Sometimes when you look at the horse, you can see wings and other times you don't. I also saw the horse walk and it didn't leave any tracks. A little man was sitting on the horse but sometimes I would see a large rolly polly or a large cricket. Any way a man, a little man, got off the horse and walked to our door and rang the doorbell. He did not tie the horse; matter of fact, the horse turned around and watched him. The huge horse was standing on soft grass but made no tracks in the grass. We answered the door and talked a bit with the man, strangely he kind of sang when he talked. Seemed like everything he said was like the song of a cricket. What he wanted to know was if we wanted a rug installed. We said we did but wanted a special kind of rug, very soft, if dirty it can almost clean itself, also it must feel soft and warm even if it is very cold outside, at night be able to help you find your bed, and we also wanted the rug to be kind of enchanted with special qualities a child would like."

The little man listened and said, "I have the very rug you are looking for."

Grandma said, "You do, where is the rug you do not even have a truck or car, you have only a horse."

The little man said, "We do not need a car or a truck, our horses and special wagons are very quiet very fast see."

We looked where the huge horse was standing and now there were four more huge horses and a wagon right there in front of our house loaded with the rugs which looked like the color and the kind we wanted. The little man took out a piece of rug from his pocket and said it had all the qualities and more that we had told him we wanted and that he could quickly install it now if we wanted him too.

Grandpa said, "How? There is no one with you, look at the wagon."

Grandma said, "Look grandpa, there are lots of little men there." Grandpa now saw all the little men who seemed to have magically appeared.

Grandpa said, "Okay, but first grandma do you like the rug, the color of the rug, the quality of the rug and is the rug okay with you?"

Grandma said, 'It's okay with me, if you like it."

Grandpa said, "It's okay with me, I like it. Let's ask the man the cost of the rug."

The man said, "It's a present for your grandchildren, Jody and Germaine, it will never grow old it will last forever, and it is a story that can be told over and over and over again. Their children can use this rug in stories forever. We can install it quickly, even now, if you want us to."

Grandma and grandpa said, "Okay put it in."

The little man and all his little friends went to work and in about an hour they were finished because the rugs were already cut to fit each room, all the rooms we had in mind to put rug in.

Grandpa said, "A very special rug was put in your room Jody and Germaine, as you can see its different just look it's different!"

"Yes" Jody, Germaine, and their parents said, "that is quite a story and hard to believe all this has happened since we were last here."

"But it has," said grandma and grandpa.

"The little man also left that special piece of rug he said was for Germaine and Jody. Only others in our family can use it, but it's special for Germaine and Jody to use till they are 21 years old. He didn't say what happens then," grandpa said.

That's not all," said grandpa as he pulled off his hat.

Germaine said, "Grandpa you're not bald anymore your hair is back, you even look more young, we didn't notice before but both of you look younger. Does your arthritis still bother you?"

Grandpa said, "No, doesn't seem to, not since we lay on the rug once in a while. That rug must be enchanted like the little man said. You know when they were putting that rug down it was funny sometimes when you looked at the people working it looked like rolly pollys were there working, then it looked like men, then crickets working, and then little men again. Strange, very strange the whole thing was, but the rug is great, we like it. When they finished we wanted to give them something, the little man said no and he walked out the door. We heard the drone of a bee, we looked in your small room Jody and Germaine and there was the two rolly polly's and two crickets. Then we heard the sound of a bee drone and the large bee first landed by them then flew around to all the rooms where the rug had been installed, then landed again by the rolly pollys and crickets. The bee then flew out the open door. Like magic, the rolly pollys disappeared, the little man, the horses and wagon all disappeared. You know, there were no horse tracks, no wagon tracks or anything, only new rug in all the rooms we wanted it in. Now that we have told you the story of the new rug, while you are here on your vacation enjoy the new rug."

"Oh we will," said Jody and Germaine and their parents. "Gosh," said Jody to her mother and father, "Grandma and grandpa had a lot happen here since we left last time, that sounds almost like a fairytale." "That's why they never told anyone else, no one would believe it," said her parents.

"But the rug is here," said Germaine.

"I know," said father. "People don't get rugs like that, they go to the store and buy them then people come and install them. They are not installed by rolly polly's and crickets, or hauled in on white horses wings and a wagon, or by little men riding white horses with wings, it really sounds like a large fairy tale. But the rug is here. Let's see what happens when we use it during our vacation."

"This is going to be a great vacation," said Germaine. "Jody, let's take that piece of rug and lay on it on that big piece of grass under the big apple trees. That should be a nice place to rest and read some of the books we brought."

"Okay," said Jody, "we can do that tomorrow. Let's go to bed now it's late."

"That's right," said their parents, "it's been a long day and a long trip here, the airplane, car, and everything. First thought lets tell grandma and grandpa goodnight and thanks for the history of the new rug." Grandma and grandpa were waiting. Grandma had fixed a light bed-time snack for everybody. Everybody enjoyed the snack, said goodnight, and turned in for the evening after such a busy day.

Jody and Germaine were in their beds in the small room and they talked for quite a while about what grandma and grandpa had said about the rug.

"That was quite a story wasn't it" said Jody.

"Sure was," said Germaine, "it's sure hard to believe but if grandpa and grandma said it, I believe it." "So do I," said Jody.

"But let's go to sleep now," said Jody. "Okay," said Germaine."

"Jody," said Germaine, "the rug is really soft isn't it?" "Yes it is, Germaine, you better lie down and go to bed Germaine. The lights are out you might trip over something." "It's okay Jody, this rug is not dark I can see everything." "It's dark Germaine," said Jody.

"It's not when you're standing on it," said Germaine. "Try it Jody." "Okay Germaine, but just to keep you quiet. Say, it's not dark on the rug, when you're standing you can see everything on the floor."

"See I told you Jody," said Germaine.

"Yeah, you're right Germaine," said Jody.

"Jody, see that white horse over there with wings on it just standing there, is it for real?" "I don't know" said Jody.

"Yes, the horse is for real," said a voice and I'm Stephan a little man from another place quite far from here, we ride here very quick on this enchanted blanket and we can go anywhere, anywhere you want to go and be back as quick. Where would you like to go? When we return you will then have a good night's sleep because I know that both of you, along with your parents, are tired from your long trip today. It will be okay to go with what you have on, pajamas are alright because the way we travel you will never get cold.

"Okay let's go," said Jody.

"Yes yes," said Germaine "I want to go! Let's go to Toyland, okay Jody?"

"Okay" said Jody.

"To Toyland we'll go," said the little man driving the flying horse, "climb on we'll be off." Jody and Germaine climbed on and off they went flying, flying high it seemed with hardly a breeze up, they went to the stars and the moon, right through the milky way, and into a wee small gate where a very small toymaker with many keys said, "Let me open the Toyland room where many toys are."

The horseman said, "Okay, but we can only stay for a short while because we have to stop at Slumberland, we have a special pass for there."

"That is no problem," said the toymaker. He opened the Toyland room. The room was beautiful with loads and loads of toys, beautiful beautiful toys, cars, boats, airplanes, dolls, dolls, dolls, small dolls, medium dolls, large sized dolls, dolls that walk, talk and even sing little songs. Airplanes that fly with turning propellers, small trains on tracks, buses, cars, motorcycles, motorcycles with sidecars, bicycles, helicopters, ships, submarines, jeeps, tanks, little kitchens with small stoves, almost any kind of toy.

Jody and Germaine said, "Toyland is great I want to come back here sometime." Jody said, "I like this place, it's good you thought to come here Germaine, but we must go now because the man driving the horse said we have a special stop to make at Slumberland and we can't be late because he is waiting okay Germaine?"

"Okay," Germaine said "all these toys are great."

Before they left the toymaker gave them each a small, very small gift. Jody received a small cabbage patch doll and Germaine received a small P-57 model airplane. They put their toys in their pajama pockets, thanked the toymaker, climbed on the flying horse and were in Slumberland very quick.

Then the horseman rode them on the flying horse right back to the little room, their bedroom, where they first started. They climbed off the horse, thanked the horseman and walked on the enchanted rug where they could see everything on the floor, then climbed right into their beds. They told each other, "that was a nice ride to Toyland," and went to sleep.

When they awakencd, cleaned, brushed their teeth, went to breakfast they took the small toys the toymaker gave them. Their parents asked Jody, "Where did you get the small cabbage patch doll I've never seen anything like that and Germaine where did you get the small P-57 model airplane?"

Both Jody and Germaine said, "We went on the flying horse to Toyland and the toymaker gave them to us when we left."

Their father and mother laughed and said "where is this Toyland?"

"Oh it's on the other side of the milky way" said Jody and Germaine. "That's pretty far isn't it?" said their father.

Then grandpa who was listening said, "No it's not so far when you have a room that's been covered with an enchanted rug, a lot of very strange things can happen and surprisingly do." Jody, Germaine, father and mother listened and agreed after recalling grandpa and grandma's story from yesterday about the rolly polly's and crickets and the installation of the rugs.

Everyone had a nice breakfast had a little walk in the fresh country air at grandpa's farm then came back a little tired. Jody's mother and father lay down on the rug to rest a while, when they awakened Jody's mother said she had had a dream that she had been shopping somewhere in a big department store in Chicago and had bought some items and had them shipped to grandma's house. She also ordered a pizza to be delivered to grandma's house. Then father awakened shortly after mother said he had a good sleep and said the rug is very comfortable. He had a dream that he had taken a long trip with an old car which broke down, so he walked to a little town and bought an old bicycle and rode it to a train station. He then rode the train to grandpa's town and brought the bicycle too. What a dream he said, but it was a good sleep.

Grandma listening and said, "It's good everybody's rested, there is something special about that rug." "Good," grandpa said, "let's go for a little boat ride"

Germaine and Jody said, "Oh boy that sounds good lets go, maybe I can catch a fish." "Okay," said grandpa, "I have good fishing poles."

Germaine's mother said, "I'll stay home with grandma, think I'll rest again on the rug and read a book for a while, the rug is very comfortable."

"That's a good idea," said Grandma "Think I'll rest a bit too."

So grandpa, Jody, Germaine, and their father went for a boat ride in grandpa's boat. Grandpa had a nice little boat with a little cabin on it; he kept it at a boat dock in town. They all drove down in Jody's father's rented car, took a fishing pole for Germaine along with some fishing gear and away they went for a good time. The little town wasn't far away and they soon were at the boat. They started the boats motor, backed out, and off for a ride they went.

Grandpa drove the boat awhile, and then father took over. Jody got to drive some, then Germaine. Germaine did not drive long because he wanted to catch a fish. So Grandpa baited the hook and gave Germaine the fishing pole. Grandpa slowed the boat down for Germaine so he could fish.

Back at the house, Jody's mother was asleep on the rug the same time Germaine was fishing and later said that she had a dream that Jody dropped her doll in the water while watching Germaine catch a fish. Mom was dreaming that Jody jumped into the water to get the doll but Jody could not swim very well and so mom told Grandma to call the coast guard for help. Grandma was sleeping on the rug to and she said she dreamed that she called the coast guard to help Jody, it all happened about the same time.

Back at grandpa's boat, Jody actually had dropped her doll in the water and jumped in to get the doll. As soon as she jumped into the water, the coast guard quickly arrived from almost nowhere and pulled her out. Everyone told Jody not to jump in deep water after a doll and that we can get you another doll. Father thought maybe there is something to this enchanted rug with both Jody's mom and grandma having dreams like that.

One good thing about the boat trip was that Germaine caught a large fish. Grandpa and Germaine cleaned the large fish Germaine caught and everyone enjoyed a good fish fry that night.

The next day Jody and Germaine took the piece of rug that was left by the little man especially for Germaine and Jody out and laid under the shade of an apple tree where Germaine wanted to read books. It was a very nice day and while reading they fell asleep on the rug. Germaine dreamed a little then awakened to see the white winged horse with the little man close by so he woke Jody.

He said, "Jody look the man with the flying horse is here and wants to know if we want to go somewhere again, where do you want to go?"

Jody thought dreamland, where everything is lovely and beautiful all the time.

"Okay," said the horseman, "hop on, let's go." Jody and Germaine hopped on the winged horse. They flew across the moon, stars, through a golden gate to dreamland. People always come and go there and experience happy things, anything they desire they can get there because its dreamland. Jody dreamed of beautiful dolls, lovely toys, kitchens, bicycles, skateboards, dishes, pans, and books, everything she could think of. Germaine dreamed of airplanes, cars, trains, boats, submarines, Batman suits, books, and bicycles, everything he could think of. Both had a wonderful time in dreamland, and then the horseman said we have to go we must get back to the enchanted rug soon. So Jody and Germaine hopped on the winged horse and the horseman flew quickly through the golden gate over the stars, the moon, and the sun, across the sky, and back to the enchanted rug. Jody and Germaine got off the winged horse thanked the horseman picked up the enchanted rug and took it back and put it in the closet of their little room.

If you ever go to grandma and grandpa's little farm be sure and look for the Enchanted Rug. It's probably still there with the winged white horse and little horseman. Jody, her parents, and Germaine talked about the Enchanted Rug for a long time and they will always remember it, especially their trip to Toyland and Dreamland.

Jody always keeps her little cabbage patch doll no one can have that it's from Toyland and Germaine always keeps his little P-57 model airplane it's from Toyland.

Toyland…

That's a very special place.

About The Author

I'm Al Vicent, originally from Michigan.
I settled in Salinas California after military service
and enjoy writing poetry to fill the vacancy of the
seconds, minutes, and hours that occur during the
days, weeks, months, years.

Printed in the United States
By Bookmasters